KU-725-971

Piccolo True Adventure series

John Gilbert
PIRATES AND BUCCANEERS

text illustrations by Edward Mortlemans
cover illustration by C. L. Doughty

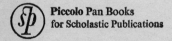

Piccolo Pan Books
for Scholastic Publications

First published 1971 by Pan Books Ltd,
Cavaye Place, London SW10 9PG
2nd printing 1976
This Scholastic edition published 1977
© John Gilbert 1971
ISBN 0 330 25209 7
Printed and bound in Great Britain by
Cox & Wyman Ltd, London, Reading and Fakenham

Contents

Pirates and Buccaneers

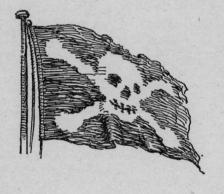

Introduction

Fifteen men on the dead man's chest
Yo-ho-ho, and a bottle of rum . . .

Everyone who has read or seen the film version of Robert Louis Stevenson's *Treasure Island* comes away with a vivid mental image of piracy – black sails against a lurid red sunset; the skull and crossbones flying from the masthead; desperados with curling moustaches and gold ear-rings swarming aboard a becalmed galleon, brandishing pistols and cutlasses; mutineers forced to walk the plank, cast adrift in an open boat or marooned on a bleak desert island; treasure chests brim full of doubloons and pieces of eight . . . No band of adventurers, not even the gun-toting heroes of the Wild West, has so powerfully gripped the imagination of generations of young readers. Even in our amazing age of space flight and exploration, with men capable of travelling to the moon and back, the long-dead pirates and buccaneers of the Spanish Main still appeal irresistibly to all who enjoy an exciting adventure story.

Who Were the Pirates?

What was the real truth? How much is fact and how much fiction? Most good tales have some factual foundation. Cowboys and Indians really existed and so too did the pirates. In fact, they have been around ever since men first took to the sea to trade, to make war and to explore – thousands of years ago.

The pirates came from many seagoing nations and over the centuries were known by many different names – privateers, sea-rovers, freebooters, buccaneers, corsairs, and filibusters. Some of them were well born, received good educations and set out with high ideals, eager to serve their God or their King. Many of them refused to admit that they were pirates at all. But the rank and file were ordinary men from all walks of life, the sons of honest tradesmen or farmers, driven to sea to escape the pointless drudgery of daily life or the miseries of poverty and unemployment. Some were deserters, desperate to escape the harsh torments of life in the Army or Navy. And at the opposite end of the scale were the criminals and misfits, frantically trying to evade the clutches of the law.

But whatever their background and upbringing, or the reasons that led them to adopt the adventurous life of a pirate, one tantalizing goal beckoned them all on – wealth. No matter how overwhelming the odds against them, there always remained the hope of plunder – money and jewels to make them rich men overnight and allow them to bask in comfort and luxury for the rest of their days. For such rewards they were prepared to endure cramped and un-healthy living conditions, mouldy food and polluted water, beatings and bullying, the miseries of gales and hurricanes. With the lure of untold wealth in store they were ready to risk their very lives.

The Pirates' Hunting Grounds

No major sea route was ever entirely free of pirates. In an-cient times it was the China Seas and the Mediterranean, focal points of the great civilizations of East and West. Pirates from Greece, from Crete, from Rome, from Turkey, and from the Barbary Coast of Africa roamed the length and breadth of the enclosed Mediterranean Sea for cen-turies. Farther north, in the icy Atlantic, the North Sea and the Channel, Vikings and privateers took their toll of peace-ful ships and settlements, even venturing inland, far up the great European river estuaries.

In the great age of European discovery and conquest, as the navigators of Spain and Portugal probed westwards to

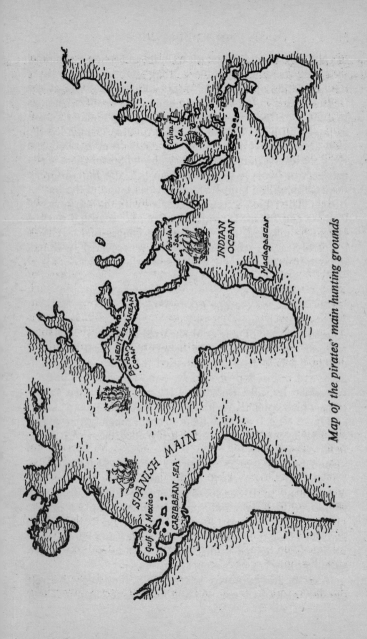

Map of the pirates' main hunting grounds

the New World and eastwards to India and the Spice Islands, the pirates travelled with them. They established their bases in the islands of the West Indies, poised to strike at the treasure fleets in the Caribbean and at the Spanish colonies in Central and South America – the region popularly known as the Spanish Main. And when Portuguese seamen led the way around the Cape to India, pirates from Europe and Asia converged in bloodthirsty rivalry wherever there was a prospect of booty – in the Arabian Sea, the Indian Ocean (especially off the famed Malabar Coast), and in the Bay of Bengal. The China Seas again teemed with the war junks of Chinese and Japanese pirates. Last of all, because it was the last to be mapped, they combed the fringes of Magellan's Peaceful Sea, the vast Pacific Ocean. Wherever ships sailed, there the pirates watched, waited and struck.

The Pirate Ships

Almost any type of ship could be used by pirates, the lighter and more manoeuvrable the better. In Classical times and during the Middle Ages they used the galley and the galleass, swift vessels propelled by oars, which could be supplemented by sails. But during the age of the great sailing ships which coincided with their own proudest years, larger and faster vessels allowed them to roam much farther afield, and the invention of the cannon provided them with deadlier fire power.

One favourite pirate vessel was the 30–50-ton sloop, a single-decked, converted cargo ship, easily stripped for offensive action. It was speedy, simple to careen (turning the ship over to repair and scrape clean of tropical marine growths), and was capable of carrying several fixed cannons and swivelling culverins. On board were a number of small rowing boats called pinnaces, which were used for navigating shallow coastal waters and rivers.

If the pirates captured a larger ship, they might convert her for their own use. A well-armed merchantman, for

example, was proof against any but a fully equipped man-of-war. It had the added advantage of being difficult, if not impossible, to identify as a pirate ship.

In the Far East, the flat-bottomed, solid junk, which was the standard seagoing vessel for thousands of years, served equally well as a pirate ship.

Life on Board a Pirate Ship

The daily round on a pirate ship must have been pretty dull, except for the rare occasions when she went into action against an enemy. The armed sailing ships of the sixteenth and seventeenth centuries were usually dirty and over-crowded. Although many of the crew slept on deck, the majority had their quarters below in the hold, among the ropes, tackle and stores, the guns and the ammunition. Here they lived, ate and slept together. It was dark, airless and, in summer, stiflingly hot. Hammocks were not generally issued and the men dossed down where they could with their few possessions.

Their food was usually adequate but the diet was monotonous – bread, biscuits, salt fish, salt meat, water and rum. On long voyages, however, or in emergencies, rations might be short. The meat and fish would go bad, the water turn brackish, the biscuits weevily. It was rare for the men to enjoy the luxury of fresh meat, fruit and vegetables. This is why the vitamin-deficiency disease of scurvy ran rife through many a crew. Add to this the normal inconvenience of seasickness and the fact that it was impossible to keep either body or clothes clean, and it can be readily understood that life below decks could be at best uncomfortable, more often unbearable.

A remarkable feature of the lives of the pirates of all times and nations is that they drew up for themselves strict rules of behaviour. They were known as Pirates' Articles and were closely observed, at risk of severe punishment. The Articles outlined the pirates' rights, duties, privileges, and punishments. Prize money, for example, was shared out in certain proportions and there were fixed rates of compensation for the loss of an eye, an arm or a leg. When a vessel was captured, quarter had to be given: that is, no prisoner, unless resisting, was to be killed; more often he would be conscripted as a member of the pirate crew. The man who first sighted a prize was awarded money or a pair of pistols. Punishments were prescribed for drunken and unruly behaviour, for cheating, for violating prisoners, and infringing safety precautions. For serious offences, such as cowardice, disobedience under fire, desertion or mutiny, the penalties included flogging or even execution.

According to these Articles, the captain was usually appointed by popular vote, yet his powers were restricted. In time of battle he had absolute authority and he received a double share of treasure. At other times he was a far less impressive figure. Though he had his own cabin, he enjoyed little privacy and ate the same food as his men. It was the quartermaster who had the right to punish minor offenders and to supervise the division of loot. He was responsible for the crew's welfare and had the doubtful privilege of leading boarding and landing parties. Other important officers and crew members included the bosun, the sailing master, the gunner, the cook, the carpenter, and the sail-maker. Perhaps the most unenviable job was that of the doctor who was frequently called upon to perform the most delicate operations in the most difficult conditions, without, needless to say, anaesthetics or pain-killing drugs.

Into Battle

The boredom of daily routine, when weeks might pass without spotting land or another vessel, was dramatically shattered when a prize was sighted. Then the ship was rapidly prepared for action, the guns, powder, balls and fuses made ready, the hand weapons shared out and the entire ship converted into an armed camp. Pirate strategy generally called for opening broadsides from the cannons, followed by bursts of small-arms fire. If this succeeded in damaging the enemy's rigging or exploding his powder magazine, the pirates would draw alongside and clamber aboard with ropes, nets and grappling hooks. Then they would close with the enemy in bitter hand-to-hand combat.

Each pirate carried an assortment of weapons. Cutlass and pistols were usually his own, but he would also be provided with other weapons as available – knives, axes, pikes, muskets, grenades, and possibly jars filled with sulphur, graphically known as 'stinkpots'. Any weapons captured from an enemy went to swell the pirates' arsenal.

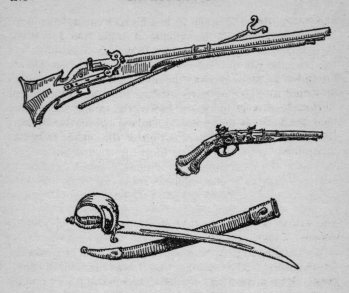

Success and Failure

Many pirates were lucky, sharing in the spoils of a plundered galleon or a looted town. If the prize was a particularly valuable one, it might include doubloons (about
£1.80), pieces-of-eight (worth roughly 22½p) and an assortment of other coins. There might be gold dust, silver
ingots and plate, jewels, precious silks, spices, and other colonial produce. More often the haul would be much more
modest. It was a calculated risk and the money was usually
soon spent. After a wild fling on shore with wine and
women, the pirates were off on a new venture, and this time
the result might be very different.

If things went badly, no victim sighted or a battle lost, the
pirate had little to look forward to. The terms on which he
had signed on clearly stated 'No purchase, no pay' – in other
words, if there was no plunder there were no wages. And
worse still might be in store – death by drowning, fire or

explosion, from the slash of a cutlass or a musket shot, from festering wounds or inhuman tortures, from starvation in a jungle or exposure in an open boat, slowly in the stinking hold of a galley or an obscure prison cell, or quickly at the end of a rope. For men who lived by the fire and sword, no mercy could be expected, neither from the enemies who thirsted for revenge nor the authorities who placed a price on their heads. Better to live for the day and agree with Captain Bartholomew Roberts who described it as 'a short life and a merry one'.

The Romance of Piracy

The writers of pirate fiction have been responsible for introducing a number of myths about pirate methods and habits. It is disappointing to learn that the real pirates normally flew a plain red or black flag rather than the skull and crossbones. But some captains did fly special emblems, including the outline skeleton known as the Jolly Roger. This term probably came from the French buccaneers' name for their red flag, the 'joli rouge'.

We have all read about 'walking the plank'. There is no evidence that this punishment ever existed. Cowards and mutineers were generally dispatched much more quickly, shot at point-blank range or tossed overboard. And the fascinating tales of 'buried treasure' also seem to be unfounded. Certainly no large treasure hoard has ever been discovered, though this will not deter the treasure seekers of the future.

The fact that not all the details of pirate fiction are historically correct does not really matter. Even some of the 'real' episodes are probably exaggerated – too bloody or far-fetched to be believed. But the journals, diaries, government papers and trial transcripts prove that the pirates did live, fight, and die much in the manner described in the following pages. There is room, after all, for both fact and fiction. Blind Pew, Jim Hawkins, Ben Gunn, and Long John Silver are unforgettable. But for sheer excitement and variety they are far surpassed by the Barbarossas, Francis Drake, Henry Morgan, Alexander Selkirk, and Blackbeard. The proof is here, in their stories.

A Pirate Glossary

Bomb Ketch   A small two-masted vessel carrying bomb-throwing mortars.

Buccaneer   A pirate; originally one of the seventeenth-century French pirates of the Caribbean, later applied to all pirates preying on shipping and settlements on the Spanish Main.

Careen   To turn a ship on her side for repairing or cleaning.

Corsair   A pirate or pirate vessel, particularly those roaming the seas off the Barbary Coast of North Africa.

Culverin   A very long land or naval cannon, first used in the sixteenth century.

Cutlass   A short, broad sword with a slightly-curved, single-edged blade, much used by pirates.

Doubloon   A Spanish gold coin whose value, once about £1.80, later dropped to around £1.

Filibuster   A pirate, especially one of the French buccaneers of the Spanish Main.

Freebooter   A pirate, originally one of the Dutch pirates of the Caribbean; literally, one who roves freely in search of plunder.

Frigate   A large, fast, three-masted sailing ship, mounting twenty-four to fifty guns.

Galleass   A heavy three-masted war vessel, larger than a galley, propelled by oars and sail.

Galley	A long, flat, one-decked seagoing vessel, once common in the Mediterranean, equipped with sails but normally rowed, often by slaves.
Give Quarter	To show mercy or avoid killing a defeated enemy.
Jolly Roger	Traditional name for a pirate flag, showing either a skeleton or a skull and crossbones; probably derived from the French 'joli rouge'.
Letter of Marque	An official document entitling a private person or captain of an armed ship to attack enemy vessels and property.
Maroon	To put ashore and leave a person on a desert island or other secluded place.
Musket	An early form of hand gun, used by sailors and soldiers.
Piece of Eight	A Spanish silver dollar, of varying value, once worth about $22\frac{1}{2}$p.
Pinnace	A small rowing-boat carried on board a larger vessel used in shallow waters.
Pirates' Articles	Written regulations defining the rights and duties of a pirate crew.
Privateer	An armed vessel, or captain of such a vessel, holding a 'letter of marque' permitting attacks on enemy ships and possessions.
Sloop	A single-masted, fore-and-aft rigged sailing ship, frequently used by pirates.
Spanish Main	The early Spanish settlements in Central and South America, but often applied to all Spanish colonies in the Caribbean.
Stinkpot	A primitive type of bomb, often

	a sulphur-filled jar, designed to explode and give out noxious fumes.
Turn King's Evidence	To earn one's freedom or a lighter punishment by giving evidence in a court of law against one's companions.
Turn Off	To hang.
Walk the Plank	To be punished by stepping blindfolded on to a plank extending from the side of a ship. Though common in fiction it was never practised by real pirates.

1

Pirates of the Aegean Sea

The Revenge of Julius Caesar

In the year 78 BC, a merchant ship, rowed by galley slaves, was following a leisurely course along the desolate and rocky coast of the Peloponnese in Greece. The square sail rigged to its single mast provided little motive power for on this warm day there was scarcely a breeze to ruffle the calm blue surface of the sea. Suddenly the master's attention was drawn to a number of low, sleek, high-prowed canoes some distance astern, and rapidly overtaking them. Escape was clearly hopeless. The sail was lowered and within the hour a horde of brutal-looking pirates had swarmed over the sides without any resistance being offered.

With much gesticulating, shouting and brandishing of weapons, the ruffianly mob drove the terrified crew members and passengers into a corner of the deck. Only one person seemed unconcerned by their threatening gestures, an aristocratic young man in fashionable clothes who sat quietly reading in the midst of all the commotion. The pirate captain strode up to him and roughly demanded his name. The young man glanced up, gave him an appraising stare, then resumed his reading without uttering a word. His insolent bearing infuriated the pirate who unleashed a volley of threats and curses. The youth remained quite unperturbed and obstinately silent.

It was the young man's travelling companion who finally broke the deadlock. This was a physician named Cinna who volunteered the information that the name of his friend was Caius Julius Caesar. He was of noble birth, as his bearing

and manner of dress suggested, and had been exiled from
Rome by the dictator Sulla. He was now bound for the
island of Rhodes where he planned to enrol in the school of

'His insolent bearing infuriated the pirate . . .'

a famous teacher of oratory. The pirate chief pondered a
moment. This young man was obviously wealthy and might
prove a valuable prize. Looming over him in a menacing
manner, he offered to set him and his servants free – for a
consideration. 'How much do you reckon you are worth?'
he mocked. Again the imperturbable young man disdained
to reply. The chief's second-in-command drew him aside
and whispered in his ear. 'A mere ten talents?' exploded the
captain. 'By heaven, we'll have double that! What do you
say, you rascal, is twenty talents a fair ransom?' At last the
young Caesar was stung into speech. 'Twenty talents?' he

drawled. 'Why, if you really knew what you were doing you'd realize that I am worth fifty talents, at the very least!' The brigand rocked back on his feet, astounded. For a captive to offer to pay several times more than had been demanded was unheard of. Fifty talents – about £8,000 – was a very considerable sum, and the patronizing young man was clearly in dead earnest. Not surprisingly, the bargain was struck without further argument.

Julius Caesar, his retinue and his fellow passengers were then bundled off at sword point to the pirates' headquarters – a cluster of sparsely furnished caves on the Greek mainland. Caesar appeared neither dismayed by the primitive surroundings nor angered by the interruption of his voyage. He had plenty of time to reflect, to read, to write and to keep his body in trim, during his captivity. He spent several hours each day running, swimming, jumping, hurling boulders, and wrestling. No author can ever have read his speeches and poems to a more unlikely audience than to this illiterate band of brigands. But though they laughed uneasily at his verses, they grudgingly paid tribute both to his learning and his physical prowess. So self-assured was his manner, even as a prisoner, that on one occasion when his sleep was disturbed by the drunken merry-making of the pirates round their campfire, he complained to their chief, who promptly quietened them down.

Yet Caesar made it quite plain that fraternization had its limits. And he was not joking when he remarked one day that if ever he met the gang again he would have them all crucified. They laughed it off as an empty threat, but were to recall his words later, to their own discomfiture.

For despite the fact that Caesar's family had difficulty in raising the ransom money after Sulla had confiscated his property, the fifty talents were paid in full and Caesar was released. No sooner had he regained his freedom than he embarked on a scheme for revenge. He borrowed four powerful war galleys, recruited 500 trained soldiers, and set sail for the pirates' hideout. He took them utterly by surprise, weak in a drunken stupor after celebrating the capture of a new prize. Only a handful managed to escape, and 350 were taken back in chains to the town of Pergamum. Their ships were scuttled and fifty talents safely returned to Caesar's purse.

Having seen his prisoners clapped behind bars, Caesar applied to the local *praetor* or chief magistrate for justice. In Caesar's view this could only be the death penalty. But the *praetor* offered unexpected resistance, resenting the peremptory attitude of this proud young man who had suddenly disturbed the smooth routine of his provincial affairs. He figured, furthermore, that if he could come to an understanding with the pirates, he could look forward both to a handsome profit and a comfortable retirement. So he delayed his decision, much to Caesar's annoyance, merely promising to take matters up with a higher authority at a later date.

Caesar had no patience with this ineffectual reply. He had already travelled hundreds of miles to intercept the *praetor* during a provincial tour of inspection. Now he galloped back to Pergamum, determined to take matters into his own hands. Pretending to be acting on the authority of Sulla himself, he gave personal orders for all the pirates to be executed without trial. The sentence was carried out before the *praetor* returned. Thirty of the ringleaders suffered the very fate Caesar had promised them months beforehand. The only gesture of mercy shown was to permit them to have their throats cut before being hoisted on to their makeshift crosses. After this interlude, Caesar, the future general and dictator of the Roman Empire, continued his interrupted journey to Rhodes.

2

Eustace the Monk

A Pirate of the English Channel

During the reign of King John of England, in the opening years of the thirteenth century, London and all the Channel ports buzzed with rumours of the daring exploits of a bold pirate, who because he had once served an apprenticeship in a monastery, was popularly known as Eustace the Monk. It was said that he was the younger son of a French nobleman and that as a result of thefts committed during his wild years of adolescence, had been outlawed from France. He had then resolved to seek his fortune – by illegal methods – on the sea rather than on land. He equipped himself with a powerful ship and a loyal crew, roaming the Channel for his victims. Soon he had acquired the reputation of being a 'master pirate'. Many people believed that his success was largely due to magical powers. It was rumoured, for example, that he could make his ship invisible at will! Be that as it may, there was no organized fleet strong enough to check his progress. He offered his services to any prince or nobleman wealthy enough to pay his price, and he recruited for his growing pirate fleet sailors, vagabonds and petty criminals from every port in Europe.

When England went to war with France, King John employed Eustace the Monk quite legitimately against the French Navy. But he soon discovered that he had unleashed a tiger, for the 'master pirate' repeatedly exceeded his royal master's instructions. Once he insolently sailed far up the River Seine, burning and slaughtering as he went. Soon any ship venturing into the Channel was regarded as fair game

and King John had no alternative but to declare him an
outlaw. Yet such was the pirate's influence that when he
next set foot on English soil, he was not only granted permission to show himself at court, but pardoned for all his
crimes and showered with gifts into the bargain! From
the proceeds he built himself a fine palace in London, sent
his daughter to the most expensive finishing school in the
land, and could, had he been so inclined, have spent the rest
of his days in luxurious retirement.

But later he quarrelled with King John and decided to
change sides. He threw in his lot with England's arch-
enemy, France. When war broke out again during the reign
of John's successor, Henry III, Eustace sailed with the
French in an invasion fleet. He was given command of the
'great ship of Bayonne', with an enormous siege engine on
deck. But by this time the English Navy was a more formidable force. The English commanders outwitted the
French, and the would-be invading fleet was scattered off the
Kentish coast. Eustace's ship was boarded by English sailors
after lime had been thrown into his men's eyes to blind
them, and the celebrated pirate was discovered hiding
ignominiously in the bilges.

His attitude towards his captors was hardly in the most
defiant pirate tradition. Abjectly, he pleaded for his life to
be spared and offered the sum of 10,000 marks (about
£6,500), promising to serve the King of England loyally for
the rest of his life. Unfortunately for him, one of his captors
happened to be a sailor who had once served under him. He
charged Eustace point blank with high treason. The
'master pirate' was promptly condemned to be executed
without trial, being given the unenviable choice of deciding
whether to be beheaded on the bulwark of his ship or across
the siege engine. According to the anonymous chronicler
who reported the episode, 'He had little desire for either, but
they still cut it off.'

The head of the pirate who had scourged the Channel was
unceremoniously stuck on a lance and displayed publicly in
Canterbury and other towns in southern England, as a grim

warning to others. It is doubtful whether the display proved much of a deterrent. Many pirates followed the example of Eustace the Monk in the centuries to come. If their names are not recorded, it is probably because they were more clever and not caught.

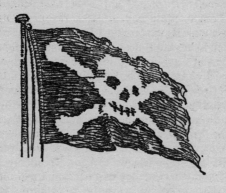

3

Arouj: the Elder Barbarossa

First of the Barbary Corsairs

On a fine, hot spring day in 1504, two great war galleys,
heavily armed and carrying a valuable load of cargo, were
proceeding along the Italian coast, not far from the island of
Elba. The ships belonged to Pope Julius II and were bound
for the port of Genoa. The two vessels were out of sight of
each other when the leading ship spotted a galliot – a small
galley propelled by oars and sail – speeding towards her.
From a distance the galliot appeared inoffensive enough,
but as she drew closer the captain of the galley was some-
what alarmed to notice that her deck was teeming with
white-clad figures wearing turbans. Suddenly it flashed
through his mind that they might be pirates – perhaps the
dreaded Barbary corsairs – yet he could hardly believe that
they would dare venture into these northern waters, so far
from their usual area of operations along the North African
coast. But as the galliot drew alongside, his worst fears were
realized.

Without any warning, a shower of arrows rained on to the
galley's deck. Minutes later, coiling ropes with grappling
hooks found their marks and dozens of black-skinned
Moors were clambering aboard. Yelling like demons, the
blades of their great curved scimitars glinting in the sunlight,
they slashed savagely at the terrified sailors, who could put
up no more than a token resistance. Soon dozens of Christian corpses lay strewn over the deck. Then the victorious
pirates rounded up the stunned survivors and herded them
roughly into the hold.

Some of the captured crew members caught a brief glimpse of the pirate chief, a stocky, muscular man of medium height, who, although of dark complexion, had a crop of red hair and a bushy red beard. Closely following him was a younger man, with similar features and also bearded. The unfortunate captain of the galley had no means of knowing that these men, brothers, were soon to become notorious throughout the Mediterranean as the Barbarossas – the Red Beards.

The Barbarossas were not content with a single prize on this fateful day. As dusk began to fall, the shape of the second Christian galley was silhouetted on the horizon, and the brothers devised an ingenious plan to lure her into their clutches. Under the menace of the pirates' scimitars, the prisoners were forced to strip and hand over their clothing. Then, innocently clad in European naval dress, the pirates went about their peaceful duties on the galley's deck. When the second vessel was within hailing distance, her captain was reassured by the sight of the crew apparently performing their normal shipboard functions. He noted with satisfaction that the galley had a Berber galliot in tow, evidently a captured prize. The two ships were almost touching each other when the red-bearded elder brother, Arouj, leapt up and barked a sharp command. Another deadly hail of arrows sped towards the second galley, causing panic on deck. The ship was boarded and the crew quickly overwhelmed. By nightfall the Moslem prisoners had been freed and the Christians chained to the oars in their place. Then Arouj and his younger brother Kheyr-ed-Din proudly escorted their double prize into the port of Tunis.

The daring and ruthless seamen who had carried out this raid were known as Barbary corsairs, so named after the Berber tribes of North Africa. They belonged to the Moslem faith, many of them descended from the persecuted Moorish community in Spain. The Moors had lived in Spain for 700 years and had made rich contributions to the country's culture – in learning, philosophy, science and the arts. Now, expelled by the Spanish King to North Africa, they nursed a

fierce hatred for Spain and the other Christian powers of the
Mediterranean, seeking vengeance for their exile through
piracy. They soon learned the skills of seamanship and acquired a reputation for courage and cruelty, preying on
Christian ships and villages, sworn to freeing their Moslem
brothers from the horrors of slavery on board Christian
galleys, and showing no mercy to man, woman or child.
They were destined to dominate the Mediterranean seas for
two centuries.

Among the earliest commanders of the Barbary corsairs
were these two Barbarossa brothers, Arouj and Kheyr-ed-
Din. Strangely enough, they were of Greek parentage but
converted to the Moslem religion. The episode of the Papal
galleys marked their first important success. At this stage in
their careers it was Arouj who issued the commands and
planned the pirates' strategy. Now he decided to enlist Turkish support against the Christian powers, and struck a bargain with the Emir of Tunis. In return for harbour facilities
and a profitable outlet for captured booty he offered the
Emir a fifth of his total haul. Some time later, when he was
notorious and powerful enough to dictate terms to kings and
princes alike, he would reduce the Emir's share to a more
modest tenth.

The Christian powers were understandably alarmed to
learn of the alliance between the Turks and the Barbary
corsairs. King Ferdinand of Spain swore to bring Barbarossa to heel and at first it seemed that he might be
successful. The pirates' bases of Oran, Bougie and Algiers,
along the North African coast, were all bombarded and re-
duced to rubble. When Arouj made a futile attempt to recapture Bougie, he had an arm shot off! But after Ferdinand's
death in 1516, the Algerians rebelled against Spain and Barbarossa at last saw an opportunity for revenge. He made a
pact with the Algerian rebel leader and marched on the town
of Algiers with an army of 5,000 men, followed by his
brother Kheyr-ed-Din, commanding the pirate fleet. The
town was taken and the Spanish garrison retreated to an
offshore island called Peñon.

Victory was sweet but Barbarossa was in no mood to share the fruits of his newly won power. One morning he strode arrogantly into the palace of the new Emir. The guards, overawed by his proud manner, scattered before him. He surprised the Emir bathing in a sunken pool in an inner courtyard, attended by a few servants and a Moorish girl playing a lute. The Emir greeted his unexpected guest politely. Barbarossa murmured that he had urgent news for his royal ears alone. The Emir signalled his servants and the girl to leave him. As the water lapped pleasantly over his shoulders he gazed up inquiringly at his visitor. Barbarossa stepped to the pool edge. 'I have a surprise for you,' he announced to the Emir, and bent down. Then before his victim could shout for help, Barbarossa had dragged him out of the bath, grabbing him round the neck with his single arm in an unbreakable stranglehold. Seconds later he flung the Emir's dead body to the floor and marched calmly out of the royal palace, as the slaves bent at his feet in homage.

Arouj was now at the pinnacle of his fortune. By common consent he was henceforth ruler of Algiers. The only thorn in his side was the small island of Peñon, where Spanish troops held out against successive Moorish attacks for thirteen years. He decided to bypass the stronghold. A decisive victory in the neighbouring province made him undisputed ruler of the whole of North Africa.

But trouble was brewing for Barbarossa on two fronts. His cruelty to his own Algerian subjects and his remorseless tortures and executions of political opponents gradually sowed the seeds of revolt. Soon he could retain power only by spreading terror throughout the land. The new Spanish Emperor, Charles V, responded readily to the Algerian rebels' appeal for help. In 1518 he sent an army of 10,000 veterans and surrounded Barbarossa, now left with a mere 1,500 loyal troops, in the town of Tilimsan. Arouj took flight for Algiers, trying to put off his pursuers by leaving his treasure behind. But the writing was on the wall. In a desolate part of the countryside he was finally cornered. There, after a fierce hand-to-hand fight among the rocks and scrub,

the once-mighty Barbarossa was killed and the pitiful rem-
nants of his army destroyed.

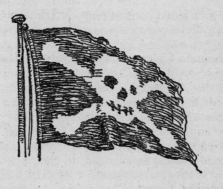

4

Kheyr-ed-Din:
the Younger Barbarossa

Corsair King of the Mediterranean

If Spain and her allies rejoiced in ridding themselves of a
dangerous foe when they killed the elder Barbarossa, their
delight was short-lived. For in the younger Barbarossa,
Kheyr-ed-Din, they were confronted by an even more formidable enemy. He was even taller and more robust than the
dead Arouj – and more intelligent as well. Taking over his
elder brother's name, property and estates, his first cunning
act was to swear allegiance to the Sultan of Turkey. In
return he received a personal bodyguard of 2,000 janissaries
– hand-picked Turkish infantrymen. He also accepted the
title of Governor-General of Algiers.

Thus assured of Turkish support, he set about building up
his private army and fleet. Soon he was strong enough to
recapture all the North African towns previously taken by
the Spaniards. And in time, though only after repeated as-
saults, he overcame the courageous Spanish garrison on
Peñon, following an artillery bombardment lasting sixteen
days and nights! The commander of the fallen fortress received no mercy, despite his heroic defence. The second Barbarossa ordered him to be flogged to death in public.

Kheyr-ed-Din now proceeded to make the western
Mediterranean a nightmare for peaceful shipping. He attacked merchant ships and war vessels alike; and when
European shipwrights taught him how to construct swift
new sailing ships, he ventured far into the Atlantic to try his

'*Barbarossa ordered him to be flogged to death in public . . .*'

luck against the Spanish treasure galleons.

The younger Barbarossa did not confine his attacks to Christian shipping. The unfortunate inhabitants of coastal villages and harbours in Spain and Italy were equally threatened. On numerous occasions Barbarossa's ships swept in to carry out a lightning raid, leaving behind a frightful trail of fire and blood. Houses were burned to the ground and hundreds of innocent farmers and fishermen slaughtered, together with their wives and children. The survivors were dragged away to be sold in Turkey or Algeria as slaves.

Barbarossa usually took no personal part in any of these terror raids, leaving them to his trusted colleagues, among whom were three celebrated and dangerous pirates high on the Spanish list of wanted men – Dragut, who later became Barbarossa's successor; Sinan, known as the 'Jew of Smyrna'; and a Christian named Aydin, fiercest of all Barbarossa's admirals, variously nicknamed 'Drub-devil' and 'Terror of Hell'.

One of Kheyr-ed-Din's boldest exploits came in 1534, when he appeared out of the blue with sixty-one galleys, sailed unopposed through the Straits of Messina separating Italy and the island of Sicily, and sacked the port of Reggio. He captured all the ships lying in the harbour and took thousands of prisoners. Not satisfied with this *coup*, he immediately sailed southwards across the Mediterranean and captured the port of Tunis, one of the last Spanish strongholds in North Africa, after a single day's naval bombardment. The Sultan, a puppet ruler of the Spaniards, fled for his life. It was a notable victory and one that Spain was resolved not to let go unpunished.

In the course of his daring raid on southern Italy, Barbarossa had heard references made in the towns of Calabria to the exceptional virtue and beauty of a noble lady named Julia Gonzago, Duchess of Trajetto and Countess of Fondi. Although reports that more than 200 poets had dedicated verses to her were doubtless exaggerated, it struck Kheyr-ed-Din that here was a prize well worth possessing. He wanted her, however, not for himself but for his royal

master, Sultan Suleiman the Magnificent. So Barbarossa
saddled a horse and galloped off to the lady's home at
Fondi, clattering through the empty streets at midnight. But
when he hammered on her doors he was infuriated to discover that, forewarned in the nick of time, she had
escaped on horseback, dressed only in her nightgown, with a
servant. What happened on the journey was never disclosed
but a reasonable guess can be made from the fact that the
supposedly loyal servant was later beheaded on her orders.
In any event, Barbarossa was left empty-handed. Bursting
with anger and frustration, he took a cruel revenge on the
innocent townsfolk of Fondi, butchering them without
mercy and burning their homes to the ground.

The Emperor Charles V was at last stung into action. In
May 1535, he dispatched a massive fleet of more than 600
vessels and 50,000 men, under the command of the famous
Admiral Andrea Doria. The next seven years were to
witness many skirmishes between Doria and Barbarossa,
and the pirate's naval supremacy was challenged for the first
time. Fortunes swayed first in one direction, then the other.
Andrea Doria won the first round when he launched an expedition which recaptured Tunis. Within a few days Barbarossa had struck back, storming the island of Minorca
and making off with dozens of ships and about 6,000 prisoners. As a sign of gratitude for this feat, the Turkish Sultan
promoted him to High Admiral of the Ottoman fleets. Each
time Doria won a local victory, his enemy retaliated by
striking at another vulnerable point in the Mediterranean –
the coast of Apulia in Italy, the island of Corfu, or the
Adriatic shore as far north as Venice.

In 1538, Barbarossa's pirate fleet won an impressive victory against the combined naval forces of Spain, Genoa,
Venice and the Papal States, this time in the Ionian Sea. The
Christian prisoners were numbered in their thousands, condemned to the galleys and the slave markets of Algiers.
Three years later Doria mustered his entire strength to do
battle once more – 500 armed vessels and 12,000 men. His
expedition met with utter disaster. A series of gales and

storms struck his fleet shortly after the army had landed at Algiers. By the time Barbarossa had put the finishing touches to the havoc caused by the elements, Doria had lost 300 officers and 8,000 enlisted men.

Barbarossa was never brought to justice. An alliance between France and Turkey saw him enthusiastically welcomed by the population of Marseilles. On the way to France he had again bombarded the unfortunate town of Reggio, and although now an elderly man, had come away with a young and beautiful Italian bride. It may indeed have been genuine love on his part, although the girl herself seems to have had little choice – her aged suitor having threatened to slaughter her parents if she refused! Yet even now time hung heavy on his hands. His pirate raids on French coastal resorts and the ruffianly behaviour of his crews soon made the French regret having invited him to be their honoured guest. But the time came when even the great Barbarossa was too old for further adventures. He spent the final five years of his life in retirement in Constantinople, rich, famous and free. He built himself a splendid sepulchre there, in which he was buried when he died in 1546.

The reign of the Barbarossa brothers was now at an end. New pirate chiefs succeeded Arouj and Kheyr-ed-Din, and the Barbary corsairs continued to terrify shipping in the Mediterranean right up to the seventeenth century. But no subsequent Barbary pirates were ever quite as notorious as the famous Barbarossas, who probably committed more daring acts of piracy than all the adventurers of the Caribbean put together.

5

Dragut

From Galley Slave to Pirate Chief

When Kheyr-ed-Din, the second Barbarossa brother, retired as an old man from piracy, his fleet was taken over by one of his most faithful officers, Dragut. Dragut had suffered in Christian hands for four years as a chained galley slave, and his hatred for all Christians was even more implacable than that of the Barbarossa brothers. By a stroke of irony, it was the Barbary corsairs' old enemy, Andrea Doria, who agreed to free him from the galley in which he was held captive. An officer who had served as a galley slave in one of the younger Barbarossa's ships recognized Dragut, dishevelled and demoralized after his years of torment. He greeted the pirate in a friendly manner, pointing out that he was in this sad plight because of the custom of war. 'Yes,' agreed Dragut. 'The luck has indeed changed!'

The sympathetic officer persuaded Doria to strike a bargain with Barbarossa, and Dragut was set free on payment of 3,000 crowns. It was a deal which Doria was to regret bitterly. Dragut's pirate fleet terrorized the shipping of Christian nations just as mercilessly as had Barbarossa's, and Doria, during his last active years, swore to bring the corsair to justice.

In 1550, Doria's ships swooped down on Dragut's base on the island of Jerba, off the coast of Tunisia. The island was strongly fortified, and was particularly convenient as a naval base because of an inland lake. This lake was connected by a narrow channel with the sea, the waterway being guarded by guns along its entire length. Dragut was well aware of Doria's plan to blockade him, but felt himself perfectly safe and well out of range of his enemy's guns. So he drew up his galleys on the shore of the lake and set his men to careening their hulls.

Doria was no less confident. He realized that to venture down the channel would be suicidal, so he decided to block its exit to the sea. Dragut would have to make an appearance sooner or later. He would simply lie at anchor and wait for the pirate to be starved into submission. Weeks passed, then months, and still there was absolutely no sign of Dragut and his fleet. Doria's patience was finally exhausted. Risking the fire power of Dragut's guns, he very cautiously edged his way through the channel and finally emerged into the lake. The passage through the channel had been an unexpectedly peaceful one, and Doria soon realized why as he scanned the empty lake. Dragut and his ships had completely vanished.

When he sailed round to the opposite shore of the lake he understood how he had been outsmarted. Recruiting several thousand local labourers to reinforce his own work force, Dragut had made them dig an escape channel through to the far side of the island, which was unguarded. When this had been completed, his ships had been towed through to the open sea and safety. He had even had the effrontery, once out at sea, to intercept and capture a galley which had been on the way with supplies and reinforcements for Andrea Doria, waiting so confidently and patiently to spring his trap!

6

Mendez Pinto and Coia Acem

A Fight to the Death

In the sixteenth century the seamen of Europe challenged those of the Orient for mastery in their own oceans. The deceptively tranquil waters of the Indian Ocean ran red with the blood of innocent sailors and ruthless pirates. But it was not always a straight contest between the forces of good and evil, especially when the leading actors were such violent characters as the Portuguese pirate, Mendez Pinto, and the Malabar Coast sea bandit, Coia Acem.

It is true that Pinto was an author and explorer as well as a pirate, while Coia Acem bragged of himself as the 'Shedder and Drinker of the Blood of Portugals'. But there was little to choose between them. As the following episode shows, when it came to crushing natives in their scramble for colonial power in the East, the Portuguese could be as brutal and savage as anyone.

One day Mendez Pinto was sailing along the Malabar Coast when his lookout spotted an open boat adrift in the empty expanse of sea. Drawing alongside, they saw a pitiful and horrifying scene. In the bottom of the boat lay thirteen emaciated figures, dead or dying of exposure. Those that were still alive were taken on board and identified themselves as eight Portuguese gentlemen and their five servants, the sole survivors of a merchant ship which had been plundered and stolen by the dreaded Coia Acem. The rest of the passengers and the entire crew had been massacred.

Pinto flew into a terrible rage and swore prompt vengeance on the famous Malabar pirate. For days he scoured

the seas for his enemy's ships, and at last he came upon them
lying at anchor in a river estuary.

The Portuguese captain decided to strike quickly and at
night. Sailing close to the enemy under cover of darkness, he
ordered his men to open fire at point-blank range on the
Malabar vessels, bringing his ship's musicians on deck to
add noise and give the impression of an even bigger attacking
force. Drums, pipes and alarm bells formed a confused and
deafening background to the night battle. The Malabar
pirates were caught by surprise. After the first devastating
broadside the Portuguese sailors boarded the enemy ships.
Two Malabar junks were sunk during the opening minutes
of the battle, and another set on fire, causing heavy casualties. The issue seemed to be settled beyond doubt.

*'Coia Acem . . . resplendent in a suit of captured
Portuguese armour . . .'*

Suddenly a huge figure appeared, silhouetted by the flames of the burning junk. It was Coia Acem himself, resplendent in a suit of captured Portuguese armour, a crimson satin coat of mail fringed with gold. His voice rang across the water as he urged on his surviving men to a final counter-attack. 'Forward, you true believers in the law of Mohamed,' he roared. 'Are you to be vanquished by these Christian dogs who have no more heart than pullets or bearded women?' His taunts aroused his men, who hurled themselves against the Portuguese in a frenzy. At the height of the furious fighting, Coia Acem and Pinto came face to face. The Portuguese captain brought his immense two-handed sword crashing down on his enemy's skull, then hacked off his legs. The battle was over. Only five Malabar pirates were left alive; 320 of them had been killed or drowned, while the victors had lost only forty-two men. Later the Portuguese reached Coia Acem's headquarters in a 'very pleasant valley, by a delicate river of fresh water wherein were a number of mullets and trouts'. But they did not pause to admire the beauties of nature. Instead they completed their cruel vengeance by burning a pagoda which was being used as a field hospital for the wounded and sick, killing all the occupants. National honour had been satisfied in the traditional pirate fashion.

7

Sir John Hawkins

An Elizabethan Sea Dog

John Hawkins was a Devon man, son of a famous father who became mayor of Plymouth. The office had been the reward for many successful years at sea, and his wealth had been built on the profits of one commodity in particular – African slaves.

Many respectable English seamen were engaged in the cruel slave trade. They took their ships down to the coast of West Africa, bought their shiploads of native men, women and children from the Portuguese traders, crammed them tightly into the dark and stifling holds, sailed across the Atlantic and sold those who had survived the crossing to the Spanish settlers on the Caribbean islands and in the towns of Central and South America known as the Spanish Main.

John Hawkins followed his father's example and became a highly successful slave trader. Queen Elizabeth knighted him for his services. In 1567, he set off on a new voyage to the Spanish Main, with six ships. He himself commanded the *Jesus of Lübeck*. Among his companions was his twenty-two-year-old cousin, who was given charge of a smaller ship, the *Judith*. His name was Francis Drake, later to become one of England's greatest naval heroes.

Hawkins sailed first to West Africa and bought more than 400 slaves. He then crossed the Atlantic and sold his human cargo very profitably in various towns on the Spanish Main. Laden with gold and silver, he turned his ships for home. But it was August, the beginning of the storm season. Two

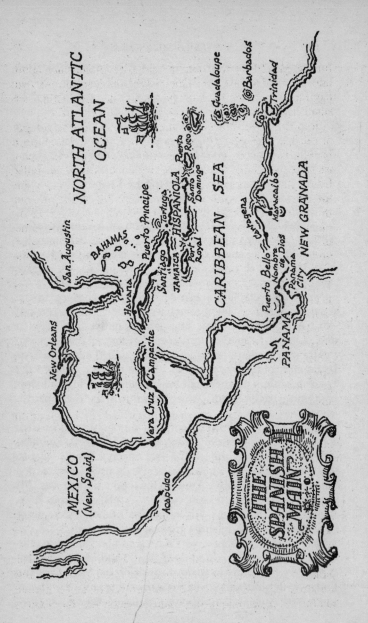

furious gales drove his battered ships north and then south into the Gulf of Mexico. One vessel was lost and his own flagship was close to sinking. Finally he shepherded his small fleet into a bay near the port of Vera Cruz.

Into this town flowed all the treasure from the interior of Mexico, then called New Spain. From here it was shipped back to Europe in the huge galleons belonging to the Spanish Treasure Fleet. There were two such fleets. One sailed from Spain to Cartagena and the isthmus of Panama. There the ships loaded gold, jewels, tobacco and coffee, moving down to Puerto Bello, where they awaited the arrival of the mule trains carrying consignments of silver from the mines of Peru. The other fleet headed for Vera Cruz, loading silver and other valuable colonial produce from New Spain, as well as goods brought across the Pacific from the Spanish Philippines and carried overland by mule train. Then both fleets, fully laden, met at Havana in Cuba; and it was as they sailed among the scattered islands of the Caribbean that the French and English pirates usually made their attacks.

Hawkins sailed into the bay only one day before the Treasure Fleet was expected. At first he was mistaken for a Spaniard. When his identity was disclosed, shrewd bargaining allowed him to dock his ships temporarily off a small island at the entrance to the harbour.

The following day thirteen large armed vessels from Spain, the famous Treasure Fleet itself, sailed in single file into Vera Cruz. It crossed Hawkins' mind that this would be a wonderful opportunity to intercept them, but he resisted the temptation. He was obviously outmanned and outgunned. He risked the loss of his own treasure, whereas the Spanish ships were empty. And to interfere with the Treasure Fleet would be interpreted as an act of war. Hawkins could not count on Queen Elizabeth's support if things went badly.

So he had to content himself with watching the Spanish galleons as they moored peacefully in the bay, only a few hundred yards from his ships. He resolved on a new plan of action. On board one of the Spanish vessels was the Viceroy

of New Spain. In order to avoid a pitched battle, Hawkins
decided to strike a bargain with him. Under this agreement
the English were permitted to remain in temporary control
of the small island where, unknown to the Spaniards,
Hawkins had already installed his cannons. To show good
faith, ten hostages were to be exchanged by either side.
Hawkins stepped out of the great cabin of the Spanish
flagship with a handsome document bearing the Viceroy's
seal, while a trumpet sounded to celebrate the truce.

Unfortunately the Viceroy had no intention of keeping
his word. During the next three days Hawkins saw un-
mistakable signs of an impending Spanish attack on the
island and his damaged ships. He sent a Spanish-speaking
envoy to protest. No sooner had the messenger set foot on
the Viceroy's flagship than the Spaniards trumpeted a call to
arms. A blistering broadside from the guns of all the Spanish ships and from the shore blasted the English vessels. An
enemy landing party then overran the cannons on the island.
Soon all those who had been fortunate enough to scramble
back on board the English ships were trapped in the centre
of a deadly concentration of gunfire.

After the initial panic had subsided, Hawkins' ship, the
Jesus of Lübeck, struck back. Accurate firing set one galleon ablaze, then another. But the *Jesus of Lübeck*, protecting the smaller *Minion*, was by now a complete wreck.
Closing in for the kill, the Spaniards sent two fireships
downwind in her direction. Hawkins ordered the crew to
abandon ship and somehow managed to get them transferred to the *Minion*. Then he steered her through the channel and out into the open sea, beyond range of the enemy
guns.

Drake, in the meantime, had succeeded in escaping in the
Judith, exactly how was never determined. Eventually he
brought the ship safely back to England. Whether he was
ordered to do so or whether he fled remained a mystery.
Hawkins bitterly accused him later of abandoning them in
'our great misery'. The *Minion* had a frightful voyage home.
At the outset Hawkins was obliged to divide the crew, 200 of

whom elected to stay behind in the jungle, risking capture by the Spaniards or a worse fate at the hands of hostile Indians. Even then the ship was appallingly overcrowded, and men died in their dozens from disease, thirst and hunger. When the *Minion* finally limped back to port, Hawkins had lost more than 300 men out of his original complement of 400, as well as all his treasure.

8

Sir Francis Drake

Scourge of the Spanish Fleets

In 1572, England and Spain were not yet officially at war with each other. Nevertheless, the colonies of the Spanish Main were regarded as legitimate fields of plunder by the 'sea dogs' of Devon and Cornwall. Especially tempting and vulnerable were the unwieldy Spanish galleons which ferried silver, gold and other precious commodities back home from the New World, across the Caribbean and Atlantic Oceans.

John Hawkins and his cousin, Francis Drake, knew these waters well. On one voyage, however, things went disastrously wrong, as we have seen, and Drake was particularly eager to return to the Indies as soon as possible to avenge the humiliation.

His immediate plan, when he sailed from Plymouth in 1572, was to raid the Spanish town of Nombre de Dios, on the isthmus of Panama. But although his small force managed to fight its way into the town, it found no spoils worth taking, the Treasure Fleet having left a few weeks previously. Drake, however, had established contact with a group of friendly Cimaroons, Negro slaves who had escaped from captivity. They put into his head an even bolder scheme. Since the galleons were beyond their clutches, why not strike a blow at the mule train itself? Guarded by only a handful of troops, these convoys carried the precious gold and silver bullion over the mountain trails and through the jungles from Panama City to Nombre de Dios, there to await the arrival of the Treasure Fleet. The Spaniards would never expect a land attack, and although the risk was considerable, the result would be spectacular.

Accompanied by seventeen companions and thirty Cimaroons, Drake marched across the isthmus, becoming the first Englishman ever to set eyes on the Pacific Ocean – the great South Sea discovered by Magellan. But the opportunity for an attack did not come till later, when they were back near Nombre de Dios. There, assisted once more by the Cimaroons, he prepared an ambush. As dusk fell, the small band dispersed themselves, hiding behind bushes and rocks on either side of the narrow trail along which the mule train had to travel. There they waited in silence.

A faint tinkling of bells was heard in the distance, heralding the approach of the mules leading the convoy, then the muffled sound of voices and the padding of hooves. One Spanish horseman rode in front of the column, others at intervals among the mules from whose sides swung the heavy rawhide sacks carrying the treasure. The tension mounted, proving too much for one over-eager English sailor, who jumped up before the signal had been given and prevented a surprise attack. Nevertheless, in the gloom and confusion, the pikes, pistols and cutlasses of Drake's men soon put the Spaniards to flight. Several men were wounded, however, and had to be abandoned. More disappointing was the discovery that the booty consisted entirely of silver and not gold. Much of this had to be jettisoned in the course of the dangerous trek back to the waiting pinnaces. Even so, there was more than £20,000 in silver to be shared out among them, and by the time he returned to England Drake was a national hero.

Five years later, in the winter of 1577, Drake sailed once more from Plymouth with five ships – no pirate raid this, whatever the Spaniards might think, but a full-scale expedition. Exactly what its true objectives were is still disputed by historians. Possibly it was to attack the Spanish west coast of South America, perhaps to discover the elusive North-east Passage, even to sail right across the Pacific to trade with the Spice Islands. But whatever his instructions, open or secret, this voyage was to make history.

Only three of the ships passed through the Straits of Magellan into the Pacific in August 1578. Drake's own vessel, the *Pelican*, was renamed the *Golden Hind*, and sailed on alone up the coast of South America, occasionally putting ashore to raid a town or village. A Spanish ship, with a hoard of gold ducats and a store of wine on board, was captured in the harbour of Valparaiso in Chile. Then the *Golden Hind* wrought havoc in the Peruvian port of Callao. It was from the crew of one of the captured ships in the harbour that Drake first learned of the existence of the great plate-ship *Nuestra Señora de la Concepción*, nicknamed the *Cacafuego* or 'Spitfire'. This ship had recently left Callao for Panama, with a valuable cargo of silver. Here was an opportunity not to be missed and Drake set off after her. Eluding two pursuers, the *Golden Hind* soon overhauled the slower Spanish vessel. According to the historian Hakluyt, who provided vivid accounts of the adventures of the Elizabethan seamen, the two ships met near Cape San Francisco, some 450 miles off the coast of Panama. Drake brought the *Golden Hind* alongside and called on the Spanish captain to surrender. When he received a defiant reply (the Spaniard mockingly referring to the English ship as an 'old tub') he opened fire.

In Drake's words, '. . . We came to her and boarded her, and shotte at her three pieces of ordinance, and strake down her misen, and being entered, we found in her great riches, as jewels and precious stones, thirteene chests full of royals of plate, four score pound weight of gold, and six and twenty tunne of silver'. Incredibly, the huge treasure ship was unarmed, and the total value of the plunder transferred into the *Golden Hind* was not far short of £200,000. Drake, in accordance with his reputation for fair dealing with his enemies, freed both the captain and his ship a few days later.

This was indeed a fortunate encounter. No prize of similar worth was sighted in the course of the long voyage across the Pacific, around the world and back to Plymouth. But when the *Golden Hind* slipped into port after her epoch-making journey, Drake was uncertain whether Queen Elizabeth would have him clapped in irons and sent to the Tower to await execution as a pirate or whether she would receive him as a hero. The Spaniards clamoured for her to declare him an outlaw, but she resisted their pressure. War against Spain could not be delayed much longer and when it came she realized that men of Drake's calibre, with his skill in navigation and fighting ability, would be needed. So she personally conferred a knighthood on him on the deck of the *Golden Hind* at Deptford.

Drake's subsequent career was full of incident, as any history book will confirm. For several years he was entrusted with keeping piracy at bay in the English Channel, a commission which he interpreted as giving him a free hand with Spanish shipping and possessions. This led to his great raid on the West Indies in 1585–6, during which his ships sacked Santo Domingo on the island of Hispaniola, Cartagena, the most important and strongly defended city on the Spanish Main, and the base of San Agustin on the coast of Florida. He lost some 750 men in the course of the campaign, most of them from disease, and took about £60,000 worth of booty. In the following year he sailed unopposed into the harbour of Cadiz, destroying several dozen Spanish ships which were assembling there as part of the great Armada to invade England. And when the Armada finally sailed in the summer of 1588, Drake, as Vice-Admiral, was one of the many experienced captains responsible for scattering the great fleet and saving his country from the consequences of a Spanish landing.

His last voyage was with the now-elderly Hawkins. The objective this time was Panama. The twenty-seven-ship expedition aimed to cut off the wealth of Philip of Spain at the source. The result was disastrous. Hawkins died at sea off Puerto Rico and Drake succumbed to fever outside Nombre de Dios a few months later. His body was lowered into the sea on January 28th, 1596.

*   *   *

It may seem strange that one of England's greatest naval heroes should be included in a book about pirates. Yet there is no real contradiction. The Spanish authorities, with whom he was locked in conflict all his life, certainly regarded him as a pirate. Some of his enemies who actually met him testified to his courage and honourable behaviour, his seamanship and his popularity with his own men; yet they feared him more than any other sailor of the Elizabethan age and continually referred to him as a pirate, the 'master thief of the unknown world'. In the legal sense, they were probably right, at least during the years when England and Spain were not officially at war with each other. Plundering and sacking cities, capturing galleons bent on lawful commercial business, these were acts of piracy, no matter how brave or idealistic the men who perpetrated them.

Drake, together with hundreds of English sea captains like him who made a living and a handsome profit from raids on Spanish and Portuguese vessels and property, argued that they were not pirates but privateers. In other words, they sailed with 'letters of marque' from their Government permitting them to attack the shipping and colonial possessions of the Catholic powers of Europe. It is a matter of record that such privateering expeditions, some fitted out by wealthy private individuals (including Government ministers), others backed by the Queen herself, were commonplace happenings, enormously profitable for all concerned, not least for those who remained safely on land yet took a share of the loot. Privateering, in fact, was considered a highly honourable occupation for a gentleman of spirit, attracting many men of noble birth and good education. Moreover, it could also be argued that it was vitally necessary for the nation's security. So the line between piracy and privateering was a slender one, usually an invisible one. Many a freelance pirate pleaded possession of a commission to excuse his deeds, and sometimes he escaped the gallows by so doing. But usually it was just playing with words. England's enemies, in any event, recognized no such fine distinction.

The conclusion must be that it all depends which side you are on. Many a wartime commander or secret agent is hailed as a hero in his own country and branded a villain and renegade by his country's foes. Drake is no exception. But if the verdict is that at some stages in his distinguished career he engaged in acts of piracy, it also has to be admitted that he was one of the better examples of that calling. Few instances of wanton cruelty emerge from the records of his life, and compared with most of the other pirates in these pages he stands out as one of the most admirable.

9

Sir Henry Mainwaring

The Scholar-Pirate

That an expensive college education and a career in piracy might go hand in hand is well illustrated by the case of the English pirate Henry Mainwaring. Well born into a land-owning Shropshire family, Henry gained a degree at Brase-nose College, Oxford, at the age of fifteen, and seemed set for a conventional law career. But he soon tired of a desk job, volunteered to serve in a regiment in the Netherlands and in 1611 decided to try his luck at sea. He was given a commission to prey on Spanish shipping in the West Indies, for which purpose he bought himself a splendid 160-ton vessel named the *Resistance*.

When the *Resistance* reached Gibraltar, Mainwaring an-nounced to his crew that he had changed his mind and that he intended to alter course and look for Spanish ships some-what nearer to home. He then headed for the port of Mar-mora on the Barbary Coast and made it his base. His gift for leadership, his navigational skill and the bravery of his loyal crew soon set him well on the road to a successful career in piracy. He captured thirty Spanish ships with valuable cargoes and became the commander of a powerful fleet, feared throughout the Channel and Mediterranean. Yet he was a pirate with a difference. His patriotic instincts would never permit him to attack any English ships – a principle he was to observe as long as he was at sea!

King Philip III of Spain tried to bribe the famous pirate to enter his service, and so did the Bey of Tunis. Mainwaring refused to be tempted. In 1614, he sailed with eight ships across the Atlantic to Newfoundland to recruit more men. Nobody dared resist him as he refitted, provisioned and armed his pirate fleet, accepting as his due a fifth of the Newfoundland fishing fleet's food supply. From the ranks of the fishermen he then enlisted, voluntarily or forcibly, about 400 men. Any French or Portuguese vessels that happened to be in the vicinity were robbed of their cargoes, chiefly wine, but there is no record of his ill-treating the crews.

While Mainwaring was away, however, Spain recaptured the pirate base at Marmora. So he simply shifted his headquarters to Villefranche in Savoy, joining forces with another English pirate of noble birth named Walsingham. Within six weeks their combined operations against Spanish shipping had earned them a small fortune – 500,000 crowns. The Spanish King now issued a large reward for Mainwaring's capture and sent out five warships from Cadiz to destroy his fleet. Mainwaring met them with three ships of his own and sent the entire squadron, badly battered, fleeing back to Lisbon. Once again Philip offered to purchase his services – 20,000 ducats (about £9,500) a year to take command of the Spanish fleet. Again Mainwaring turned him down.

Eventually King James I was obliged, under French and Spanish diplomatic pressure, to put a stop to Mainwaring's Barbary Coast adventures. He offered the pirate a free pardon if he agreed to terminate his unlawful activities. Mainwaring did not hesitate: after all, he had no quarrel with his own monarch. He sailed home with two ships to Dover and gratefully accepted the royal pardon, on the grounds that 'he had committed no great wrong'!

Honours were now showered on his head. First came a knighthood, then an appointment as Gentleman of the King's Bedchamber, followed by the post of Lieutenant of Dover Castle and Deputy Warden of the Cinque Ports. In 1623, he was elected Member of Parliament for Dover. A wealthy man in his own right, he married an heiress. Later he went back to sea for a while and rose to the rank of Vice-Admiral.

In return for these favours, Mainwaring offered his services to the Crown by assisting in the search for pirates. His
first-hand experience proved invaluable. He wrote a book,
dedicating it to the King, in which he outlined the history of
the Barbary corsairs and other pirates and suggested prac-
tical measures for their suppression. He explained in detail
why men took to this way of life, pointing out that Ireland
was one of their favourite hideouts and recruiting centres.
He also suggested how they might be deterred. In his view,
one reason for the spread of piracy was that sentences were
not severe enough. Although he did not advocate hanging,
he deplored the custom of granting free pardons (he himself
was well out of range of the law by now) and suggested
captured pirates might be usefully employed, in the manner
of galley slaves aboard, in patrolling the coasts.

There is no evidence that Mainwaring's sensible advice
was taken. The efforts of the Stuart kings to suppress piracy
were not noticeably successful, and there were plenty of desperate men, less patriotic and honourable than Mainwaring,
who made certain that the oceans of the world remained
highly dangerous for sailors and shipping for many years to
come.

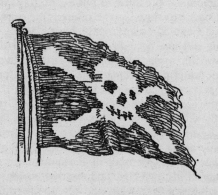

10

Pierre le Grand

A French Buccaneer

Pirates through the ages have been called by a variety of names, usually depending on their nationality. The pirates who plundered Spanish shipping and coastal settlements in the Caribbean during the seventeenth century were generally known as 'buccaneers', 'filibusters', or 'freebooters'. Although each term has a different origin, the distinction between the activities of all these men was very slight. They were all pirates, and their original base was the tiny West Indian island of Tortuga, which lay off the north-east coast of Hispaniola.

The first settlers in Tortuga were French Huguenots, freelance pirates from Dieppe, Brest and St Malo, eager to make a fortune from the galleon traffic of the New World. At first they brought their vessels in for careening and refitting to remote coves along the northern coast of Hispaniola itself; but the Spaniards soon whittled them out and drove them across the narrow stretch of sea to the turtle-shaped island from which was derived its name, Tortuga. It was only four miles wide and about twenty-two miles long. The men who settled here called themselves the Brethren of the Coast, and were united in their implacable hatred of the Spaniards. In time they were joined by desperate men from other Protestant countries, England, Ireland, Scotland and Holland. They were of all classes, backgrounds and temperaments – fugitives from justice and the Spanish Inquisition, deserters from the armed forces, or adventurers looking for excitement and quick fortunes. Later

they were joined by women, and in time they established a
small but thriving community, governed by strict rules
which enforced discipline and guaranteed common rights. It
was a continual thorn in the side of the Spanish Government.

The narrow, triangular-sailed, 'lateen-rigged' boats which
the settlers built from local timber were called by a Dutch
name – *flei-bote* or *frei-bote* – from which was taken the
English term freebooter, and its rough French equivalent
flibustier (which the English simplified to filibuster).
Strictly speaking, these were the sailors proper, who made
their living from their activities at sea. Those settlers who
elected to stay on land and hunt wild cattle and pigs were
known as *boucaniers* or buccaneers – from the French word
boucan, an open grill over which was placed a wooden
hurdle where strips of meat were smoked and salted. But in
due course all those who made a livelihood from sea piracy
came to be known as buccaneers.

One of the earliest of the French buccaneer captains was a
man named Pierre le Grand. In many ways he was not typi-
cal of the Tortuga pirates, being by all accounts more intelligent and civilized, and not at all addicted to the favourite
leisure occupations of his colleagues: women, drinking and
gambling. His famous escapade occurred in 1665, in the
waters to the west of Hispaniola. He had been cruising in a
small open sloop, with a crew of twenty-eight, hoping to
waylay a Spanish vessel. After several weeks at sea, with
food and drink almost exhausted, the ship was in a sorry
state, thanks to the battering it had received from the
elements. So le Grand and his men were near despera-
tion when one evening, as the sun was dipping below the
horizon, they spotted the silhouettes of a large convoy of
ships.

Le Grand remarked that one of the vessels had strayed far
behind the others and was losing ground every minute. He
had already identified them as Spanish treasure galleons and
he made an instant decision. They would attack the straggler. Though the odds were doubtless against them, they had

'They clambered aboard, pistols and cutlasses in their hands'

nothing to lose in their desperate plight. He explained his
plan of attack to his weary men, and so that there could be
no risk of anyone not giving of his best, he ordered them to
drill holes into the sides of their sinking boat. There could
be no retreat.

Within a couple of hours they were alongside the galleon,
unobserved in the darkness. They scuttled their boat as arranged and then, removing their boots and using every foot-
hold they could find, either with or without ropes, they
clambered aboard, pistols and cutlasses in their hands. The
sailor standing watch and the steersman were the first to be
silently overpowered, bound and gagged. Through the
lighted windows of the poop cabin le Grand watched the
unsuspecting Spanish admiral playing cards with three of his
officers. He ordered most of his men below to the crew's
quarters, urging them to try to enforce surrender rather than
open fire. Then, with four companions, he burst into the
cabin and levelled pistols at the heads of the astonished card
players. 'I demand that you surrender to me immediately
both your persons and your ship,' he ordered the admiral.
His finger twitched at the trigger as the Spaniards, speechless
with fright, stared at their visitors.

Suddenly the silence was shattered by shots ringing out
from below decks. Instinctively the admiral and his officers
made movements for the door. Le Grand fired, his colleagues followed suit, and the four Spaniards fell dead.
Below, the sleepy crew members were putting up a token resistance, but as soon as le Grand and his companions appeared, they surrendered. The dead were tossed overboard,
the wounded attended to, the prisoners locked up. When the
galleon was searched, the pirates found, to their delight,
treasure exceeding their wildest dreams – six chests bursting
with gold and many other valuables. Next day le Grand announced his decision of sailing the galleon back to Dieppe
and giving up his buccaneering . Five men who preferred not
to join him were put ashore at Port Royal in Jamaica. The
rest were content to return home to Europe with their captain, all of them now rich men. Le Grand retired from

piracy, as he had pledged, and was never apprehended for this, one of the most daring exploits in the history of buccaneering.

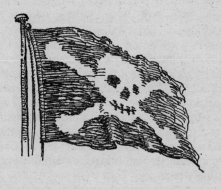

11

François L'Olonois

The Bloodthirsty Buccaneer

The French pirate captain François L'Olonois, if the stories are to be believed, was the most vicious and blood-thirsty of all the Tortuga buccaneers, worse even than the other celebrated pirate, Montbars the Exterminator! L'Olonois really deserves no more than a passing mention, for his record seems to have been one long series of brutal tortures and slaughters. So bloody is the story that one begins to suspect that no buccaneer can have been quite so unremittingly bad.

Although he was certainly quick-witted and cunning, he cannot have been much of a seaman! The first ship he commanded was wrecked in a storm; so was his second. On this latter occasion, he was driven ashore and all his men were efficiently wiped out by Spanish soldiers. To escape a similar fate, L'Olonois smeared his body, face and clothing with the blood of his comrades and lay down among the corpses, pretending to be dead. His ruse succeeded and after recuperating in the forest, he appeared walking boldly through the Spanish-governed town of Campeche, dressed in Spanish clothes. He managed to persuade some slaves to steal him a canoe and escaped with them to Tortuga.

His later adventures on the Spanish Main were somewhat more successful. Commanding eight ships and a strong landing force, L'Olonois bombarded and captured the Venezuelan town of Maracaibo, torturing his prisoners on the rack to extract information from them about hidden treasure. He then sacked and burned the town of Gibraltar, on the other side of the lake, seizing some 260,000 pieces-of-eight, an immense haul which he and his men had no trouble in spending in a matter of weeks.

The next raid, on the coast of Nicaragua, was far less rewarding. His men fell headlong into a Spanish ambush and only a few of them were able to fight their way clear. It was during the attempted escape from this ambush that L'Olonois is said to have perpetrated the deed for which he was ever afterwards remembered with dread – tearing out the heart of a Spanish prisoner who had chosen to remain obstinately silent under his none too gentle questioning. The episode was a gift to artists, who depicted it in much gleeful detail, whilst professing to be shocked. Whether it actually happened or not – for even in those days rumours could fly around, without the aid of newspapers – the Spanish authorities were now really out for his blood. And the end, when it came, was singularly appropriate. Shipwrecked yet again during a storm in the Gulf of Darien, and staggering ashore in a dazed condition, he was taken prisoner by a primitive tribe of Indians. Perhaps even they knew something of his reputation. In any event, they proceeded to tear him limb from limb, roasting the pieces in their fire and scattering the ashes so that no trace of him remained.

12

Sir Henry Morgan

The Buccaneer from Jamaica

In 1655, a force of English privateers captured the West Indian island of Jamaica. During the next forty years Jamaica, with its disreputable capital of Port Royal, replaced the French buccaneer island of Tortuga as the leading pirate base in the Caribbean. Its capture gave a special boost to the English buccaneers, of whom Henry Morgan was by far the most notorious.

Little is known of Morgan's early years, except that he was born in Wales, the son of a farmer, and that he seems to have run away to sea instead of continuing his education. He joined the Caribbean buccaneers while still in his teens, raiding Spanish ships and settlements and serving under the Dutch Captain Mansvelt. The Dutch pirate was a well-respected man, notable for being the first commander of an international force of buccaneers. In one raid on the island of Curaçao, then occupied by Spain, Mansvelt was captured and condemned to death. Morgan, still a young man, was chosen to succeed him and had soon collected a powerful pirate fleet of his own.

He proved himself a daring seaman and a courageous leader of men, the most talented adventurer since Drake. But unlike Drake, there was a cruel streak in his nature which led him to commit violent crimes against many innocent people during an otherwise distinguished career. Yet this did not prevent him being awarded a knighthood and high office!

The young Morgan soon found a staunch ally in

Governor Modyford of Jamaica, who saw this talented and ruthless adventurer as likely to perform a useful function. Spain was no longer the official enemy, for England was

'*Morgan's men spared nobody standing in their path*'

now on the brink of war with her former allies France and Holland. Morgan's pirate fleet might help defend Jamaica against surprise attack from French or Dutch bases in the West Indies, while his privateering exploits against the Spanish could prove immensely profitable both to Jamaica and the Governor himself.

So it was the Governor of Jamaica who organized Morgan's first large raid in 1668 on the town of Puerto Principe in Cuba. With 500 men, Morgan marched inland from the coast for twenty-four hours, sacking the town after bitter house-to-house fighting. But the amount of plunder was so

small that Morgan had to promise his discontented men a
share in a more profitable enterprise. He decided to assault
the Central American mainland itself, beginning with the
strongly fortified city of Puerto Bello, on the coast of
Panama.

Morgan, with 400 volunteers, landed from canoes in
darkness and advanced on the town which was guarded by
three forts. Two of these surrendered immediately when
they found themselves surrounded by a horde of yelling,
pistol-brandishing pirates. The third fort proved more
troublesome. It was commanded by the Spanish Governor,
who refused to lay down his arms and underlined his intention to fight by sending a cannon blast over the pirates'
heads. Morgan decided to bypass the fort and to concentrate
on the town itself. Already roused by the sound of the firing,
the inhabitants were running through the streets in panic,
some of them trying to hide their valuables before the
pirates arrived. They would have been wiser to stay indoors
for Morgan's men spared nobody standing in their path.

There was a faint hope for the townsfolk as long as the
fort held out. Realizing that a conventional frontal attack
might result in heavy casualties, Morgan adopted more
devious measures. He rounded up a group of priests and
nuns and forced them to carry scaling ladders across the
open ground surrounding the fort, covered by the Spanish guns. The Governor faced a frightful choice as Morgan's
men advanced in the wake of their innocent captives. He
could not afford to hesitate. Ordering his soldiers to open
fire, he watched the black-clad figures crumpling to the
ground. Even their sacrifice was in vain for Morgan's men
were soon at the foot of the fortress walls and storming the
parapets. When they were close enough they tossed fireballs
and pitchers of powder over the top. Under cover of a screen
of fumes and smoke they then closed in for hand-to-hand
combat and wiped out the entire garrison, including the
Governor. The town of Puerto Bello was now at their
mercy, but none was shown. Churches and houses were
burned and ransacked, men, women and children slaugh-

tered. And this time the loot was well up to expectations. When Morgan returned to Jamaica with his plunder, having lost only a few dozen men, the Governor had no choice but to welcome him as a popular hero.

Little time was wasted in preparing for another expedition. This time the choice fell on the unfortunate twin towns of Maracaibo and Gibraltar on Lake Maracaibo, already sacked by L'Olonois. It began with a near disaster. Morgan was banqueting his officers on board the frigate *Oxford* when a colossal explosion shook the ship's magazine and disabled the vessel. About 200 men were killed or drowned, and of the officers only Morgan and the men immediately next to him survived. Morgan himself was dragged unconscious from the sea.

Despite this inauspicious start, the assault on Maracaibo was successful. Morgan's men occupied the town for three weeks and were permitted to commit every outrage imaginable on the inhabitants. Gibraltar was also taken and plundered, but when Morgan crossed the lake to the now deserted Maracaibo he discovered that his escape channel had been blocked by three Spanish warships. Morgan prepared to fight his way out. He had captured three ships on the lake and out of one of them he constructed a fireship, complete with faked gun-ports and straw-stuffed dummy sailors. Then he filled the hold with explosives, lit the fuses and set the ship dead on course for the largest of the three warships. The first warship was set on fire and exploded. The officers of the second ship panicked and ran her ashore, then scuttled her. The third vessel was captured.

Morgan was now a wealthy man and a national hero. For a while he seemed contented to lead an easy life as a planter on Jamaica. But he was tempted into one last venture against the Spaniards, the largest and boldest of his career. With Spanish ships continually raiding English vessels off the north coast of Jamaica, Morgan was handed an open commission to attack all Spanish shipping, stores and towns in the Caribbean. Typically he decided to carry matters a stage further. He would strike at the heart of the Spanish

Main itself, at the rich fortified city of Panama. The town lay on the Pacific shore of the isthmus and Morgan knew that his only hope of success lay in attacking it by land from the rear.

It was New Year in 1671 when Morgan brought his powerful fleet to anchor at the mouth of the Chagres River. His advance landing party soon clashed with the Spanish and captured the fort of San Lorenzo. Leaving a garrison in the fort to cover his rear, Morgan set off up the river with seven sloops and an assortment of small boats and canoes. He knew the dangers involved. The river was navigable by large vessels only for about forty miles. At some point they would have to make a landing and continue the journey across the isthmus through impenetrable jungle. He counted on this part of the expedition taking six days; in fact it took them nine, and it proved to be a nightmare journey. His 1,400 men were plagued by sticky heat, by hordes of ants, mosquitoes and spiders and by their fear of the unknown. At night they were petrified by the roaring of savage wild animals; they were dropping from fatigue, weak from the effects of dysentery and starvation. For the jungle tribes had somehow been forewarned and had silently vanished among the trees and undergrowth, giving them no opportunity to attack and obtain vital food and water. By the sixth day they were gnawing at their leather belts. Then they stumbled on a supply of corn and this gave them strength to struggle on. Three days later a scout excitedly reported sighting the spires of Panama and soon they were gazing down at the little town, and beyond it the blue Pacific.

By now the buccaneers were in poor shape and Morgan refused to risk a frontal attack. Cleverly probing the weak points in the city's defences, he drew the Spanish troops out into the open, three miles outside the town. In an effort to throw the attackers into a panic, the Spaniards set loose a herd of several hundred wild bulls. But the accurate fire from the English muskets panicked the animals instead, and those that were not shot dead thundered back in the opposite direction, scattering the Spanish cavalry drawn up in their rear. The battle lasted several hours, with both sides fighting gallantly. Eventually the Spanish forces turned and fled, pursued into the defenceless city by the exuberant buccaneers. The strongest town in Central America had fallen. For twenty days Morgan allowed his men to plunder the city unopposed. At one point, fire broke out, though whether it was started by the English or on the orders of the Spanish Governor was never made clear.

Morgan was well aware that he was in an exposed position. To prevent his men getting so drunk as to be unable to defend themselves against a possible counter-attack, he forbade them to drink any wine, pretending that the Spaniards had poisoned it before leaving. The attack never came but there was no point in remaining. After capturing a number of ships in the Gulf of Panama, Morgan marched his men back through the jungle to Chagres, where the loot was shared out. Some of it was lost on the way and when it was counted most of the men found to their dismay that they had received the equivalent of only some £10 apiece. Morgan sailed off in his flagship with the greater part of the plunder, although nobody proved that he had deliberately cheated them.

Back in Jamaica, Morgan was wildly acclaimed for his bold escapade. But when the news filtered back to Spain, the Government protested so loudly to Charles II that he felt obliged to arrest the famous buccaneer and bring him back to England in irons to stand trial. Fortune was still on his side. Friends interceded for him and the trial never took place. After three years of uncertainty he received a knighthood and was sent back to Jamaica as Deputy Governor! There he lived quietly for fourteen years, helping to hunt down pirates in his turn, and dying there in 1688.

Four years later the seedy town of Port Royal was shaken by a violent earthquake. Half of the port sunk into the sea and thousands of people were drowned. Sailors later claimed that they could hear bells tolling from beneath the waves, caused by their anchors getting caught on submerged steeples! And the colourful reputation of the old pirate haunt has since attracted many treasure seekers, who have recently begun excavations in the harbour of the prosperous new city of Kingston which was built on its site. So Port Royal may still have secrets to reveal.

13

John Avery

The Arch-Pirate

By the end of the seventeenth century the great days of buccaneering in the Caribbean and on the Spanish Main were
over. European exploration had opened new trade routes
and many buccaneers moved their activities eastwards to the
Indian Ocean. The eastern seas had long been monopolized
by Arab seamen and merchants. Their ships, plying back
and forth between the Red Sea, the Persian Gulf ports and
India, held out promise of booty as valuable as any that had
been carried by the Spanish galleons in the Caribbean.
Furthermore, they were far less strongly armed and defended. In addition to these, there were the lumbering East
Indiamen – merchant ships owned by the Dutch and British
East India Companies – which could be counted upon to
provide rich hauls of Oriental commodities. A pirate could
make an easy fortune in these waters ... if he was fortunate!

One of the first of the pirates to terrorize shipping in this
area was John Avery, a Plymouth man who operated from
bases in Madagascar, off the south-east coast of Africa, and
in the nearby Comoro Islands. Some of his fellow sailors
nicknamed him Long Ben, probably because he is said to
have been rather fat, with a jolly red face. Others simply
called him the 'arch-pirate'. The novelist Daniel Defoe used
him as a model for the hero of his book *Captain Singleton*,
and Charles Johnson, who wrote *A General History of the
Pirates*, made him the central character in a play which was
produced at Covent Garden in London in 1712. It was called

The Successful Pirate, yet Avery, however successful he may have been during his short pirate career, almost certainly lost his fortune and died in poverty.

In 1694, John Avery was sailing master of the armed privateer *Charles II*, with forty-six guns and a crew of 130. She was bound for Corunna, having been hired by the Spanish Government to attack the French in the West Indies. The crew, however, was in mutinous mood, having seen little plunder and consequently no pay for eight months. The resourceful Avery easily talked them into turning the captain and his supporters off the ship and electing him instead. The ship was then renamed the *Fancy*. Avery took her round the Cape and captured a French pirate ship. He enlisted fifty-two of her crew, leaving a letter which he requested should be delivered to the next English ship in the area. This, for the benefit of the authorities at home, recounted his version of the mutiny, declared his intention of seeking his fortune at sea and boasted that he had never harmed, nor ever proposed to harm any Dutch or English vessel. He conveniently excluded three English ships which he had already plundered and burned in the Cape Verde Islands.

His intended victims were ships belonging to the Great Mogul of India and he lay in wait for them in the Red Sea. Here he was joined by another notorious English pirate named Thomas Tew, in the *Amity*. One night a convoy of twenty-five Indian or Moorish vessels (the term 'Moor' was then used to describe anyone of the Moslem faith) slipped past the pirate fleet from the port of Mocha. Avery and Tew gave chase, and two of the vessels were overtaken. One, the *Fateh Mahomed*, put up a stout resistance against the *Amity*, and during the engagement Tew was killed. Avery's *Fancy* finished off the Moorish ship and found £50,000 worth of gold and silver on board. He then took on the larger Moorish ship, the *Gunsway*, three times the size of the *Fancy*, with sixty-two guns and carrying 600 passengers and crew.

The *Gunsway*'s opening broadside scored a direct hit on

the *Fancy* and killed twenty men. Both vessels then fought
an hour-long gun duel, until a shot from the *Fancy* split the
Gunsway's mainmast. Taking advantage of the confusion
aboard the larger ship, Avery brought the *Fancy* alongside
and prepared to board. It was a calculated risk for the
Indian crew members were armed with scimitars and were
more than a match as swordsmen for their English opponents. But the sight of the pirates swarming over the sides
caused panic and the crew rushed for the hold, led by their
captain. One story tells how he rounded up a group of Turkish girls who were being taken back to India as concubines,
put turbans on their heads and tried to force them up the
ladders to fight the pirates. Their fate was the same as for
all the others who survived the savage battle, men and
women alike, including an aged relative of the Great Mogul
himself. Rape and slaughter were the order of the day, and
the treasure, in gold, sequins, pearls, silks and damasks, was
estimated at £325,000. Each member of Avery's crew received about £1,000 and Avery, as captain, took the customary double share.

Some reports said that Captain Avery captured and
married the youngest daughter of the Mogul, though this
was never confirmed. The loss of two valuable vessels and
the terrible accounts of looting and bloodshed so infuriated
the Mogul and alarmed the merchants of India that the
property of the British East India Company was threatened
with destruction. John Avery was now a wanted man. In the
general pardon offered at that period to a number of pirate
captains, only his name and one other, that of the celebrated
Captain Kidd, were missing. He decided to divide his fleet
and leave the scene of action, setting course for New Providence in the Bahamas. Once arrived, he made sure that the
new Governor would protect him and allow him to leave
and enter port at will. In return for this favour he offered the
ship (but not the plunder) plus twenty pieces of eight and
two pieces of gold from each man on board. Even in those
days £900 was a tidy sum and the Governor agreed to the

bargain. But he never got the *Fancy*. She was driven
aground in a gale and was soon a total wreck. Only her
guns were salvaged.

The East India Company now doubled the English
Government's own reward for the capture of Avery and his
men. The Governor of Jamaica, less cooperative than his
colleague in the Bahamas, turned down the sum of £20,000
in return for a general free pardon for the crew, and twenty-
four of the pirates were captured, six to be hanged. Avery
himself, with nineteen companions, hired a sloop and took it
back to Ireland. The ship was sold and the crew dispersed.
Some were later captured and turned King's evidence –
buying their freedom by informing on their comrades – but
Avery the 'arch-pirate' was never caught. He made his way
back to Bideford in Devon, his original home ground, and
there took on the assumed name of Bridgeman. He is reported to have made contact with some merchants from
Bristol who descended on him and relieved him of his dia-
monds and gold cups for bargain prices. Obviously they
cheated him, knowing full well that there was a price on his
head. Soon he was destitute and starving, dying in obscurity
at Bideford, 'not being worth as much as would buy him a
coffin'.

14

William Kidd

Privateer or Pirate?

No pirate in history, insist the stories and ballads, was half so villainous, greedy or bloodthirsty as the notorious Captain Kidd, none responsible for more innocent suffering nor so richly deserving to be hanged for his crimes. Moreover, so rumour has it, the colossal amount of treasure which Kidd accumulated in his lifetime was never properly accounted for, and it therefore stands to reason that he must have buried it in secret. Yet 270 years have passed since Kidd was hanged at Execution Dock and, despite many searches, not a single gold coin or precious stone has ever come to light. Once again, the legend and the facts are probably poles apart.

In Kidd's case, however, the truth has become almost as misty as the myth. No pirate has been the subject of so many articles and books, yet no two authors seem able to agree on their verdict. One calls him 'a worthy, honest-hearted, steadfast, much-enduring sailor'; another berates him as 'a third-rate pirate and a fourth-rate gentleman'; a third remarks acidly, 'If Kidd's reputation was in just proportion to his actual deeds, he would have been forgotten as soon as he had been "turned off" at Wapping Old Stairs'. As for his trial, the experts are just as evenly divided. Some consider him guilty and justly sentenced, others believe that he was 'framed', the unfortunate victim of bribed informers and political intriguers. 'For my part,' protested the prisoner himself, 'I am the innocentest person of them als.'

The interesting part of William Kidd's odd story begins in

1695 when he was already fifty years old and occupying a fine house in New York with his wife and children, an honoured and prosperous colonial citizen. He had been born in Greenock, Scotland, and had spent many years at sea both as an honest trader and a privateer against the French. New York and other ports on the east coast of America were known to have grown rich largely on the proceeds of piracy in the Red Sea and Indian Ocean. The famous pirate captain Thomas Tew had wined and dined freely with the Governor of New York. But eventually the exploits of the Madagascar-based English and American pirates brought such violent protests from the merchants of the East India Company that the Government was forced to take action. In 1695 the Earl of Bellomont was appointed as Governor of New York, Massachusetts and New Hampshire, and, determined to deal with the problem of piracy, he fitted out a private pirate-hunting expedition. On his recommendation, the English King appointed 'our trusty and well-beloved Captain Kidd' to take command of it.

Bellomont himself put up four-fifths of the money required (£6,000) to find Kidd a vessel, the 284-ton, 34-gun privateer *Adventure Galley*. But behind the scenes a number of other people expressed an interest in the venture, and it is obvious that they were not so much concerned with catching pirates as with grabbing a share of the plunder that Kidd was expected to bring home. It was later revealed that the secret backers included such prominent Whig politicians as the Lord Chancellor, The First Lord of the Admiralty, the Master of the Ordnance and a Secretary of State.

Officially, ten per cent of the profit was to go to the King, according to tradition. Of what was left, sixty per cent was for Bellomont, fifteen for Kidd and the other backers and an unusually low twenty-five per cent for the crew. Of course, as far as the crew was concerned, it was the old principle of 'no prey, no pay', and this was to lead to trouble.

Kidd was handed two separate commissions. The first was a 'letter of marque', issued by the Government and entitling him to seize any ship flying the French flag. The second

authorized him to capture certain pirates, including the renowned Thomas Tew of Rhode Island. It seems likely that
Kidd accepted both commissions at face value, little sus-
pecting that he was being used to help line the pockets of
prominent men who could not afford to have their names
mentioned or their reputations tarnished.

Kidd had some difficulty in recruiting a crew for the
Adventure Galley. He lost some men in England to the
press gangs and had to replace them in New York, but not
before giving them a private pledge that their share of any
plunder would be the standard sixty per cent. Then, in September 1696, the *Adventure Galley* set sail for the Red Sea,
with 155 men on board.

The full facts of this momentous voyage never became
known. It was three years before the *Adventure Galley*
berthed again at Long Island, by which time the fate of her
captain was sealed. But by piecing together undoubted facts,
disputed evidence and mere hearsay, there emerges a fascinating story.

For a year after sailing Kidd appears to have met with
little luck. There were no French ships waiting to be taken
off Madagascar or the Indian coast, and since there was no
plunder the crew had to go without pay. The ship was in
poor shape, provisions running low and the men in ugly
mood, threatening mutiny. One of the chief agitators among
the crew was a gunner named William Moore, who was especially critical of Kidd's handling of the ship. One day, as
Kidd was pacing the deck, Moore made threatening gestures
with a chisel. Kidd turned on him furiously, accused him of
conspiring mutiny and called him a 'lousy dog'. 'If I am,'
rejoined Moore, 'then you have made me one!' At this Kidd
lost his temper, picked up an iron-hooped wooden bucket
and flung it at Moore's head. The next day Moore died of a
fractured skull. Whatever the provocation, the incident was
to prove fatal for Kidd as well as his victim.

It was at this critical point that Kidd, perhaps under pressure, seems to have made a momentous decision. Rather
than waste more time aimlessly chasing pirates, he would

turn pirate himself. Yet even then his luck does not appear
to have changed much. Several small trading vessels were
captured and some survivors testified to acts of cruelty,
though these were never conclusively proved. It was not
until January 1698 that Kidd took a really valuable prize in
the shape of a 400-ton Armenian vessel named *Quedagh
Merchant*. Another Armenian ship, the *Maiden*, was captured at the same time. The loot, in the form of gold, silver,
jewellery, silk and other goods, was considerable, and it was
shared out after Kidd had transferred his flag from the cap-
sizing *Adventure Galley* to the *Quedagh Merchant*. But, according to Kidd, most of his crew then mutinied and
deserted him, taking with them the greater part of the plunder. They also took his log book, which Kidd gave as the
reason for his not being able to produce a clear account of
his voyage. Either Kidd's version of events was true or the
amount of loot was not nearly as much as had been rumoured. Far from returning home with over a million
pounds' worth of treasure, the real amount was between
£15,000 and £20,000, hardly a fortune, considering how
many people claimed a share in it.

By this time the rumours of Kidd's piratical exploits had
reached England and orders were put out for his immediate
arrest. The news astounded Kidd, and from his subsequent
actions it seems that he felt confident not only of being able
to clear himself of the charge, but also of persuading his old
friend Bellomont to stand by him. He was deluding himself
on both counts. Bellomont had strict orders to arrest him as
soon as he showed himself in New York. Kidd had left the
Quedagh Merchant in Hispaniola and now arrived back in
America in the sloop *San Antonio*. On the way he left some
chests, presumably containing treasure, with a friend named
John Gardiner who owned a small island off the eastern end
of Long Island. Kidd dispatched a letter to Bellomont, announcing his arrival and asking to see him in Boston to
establish his innocence. Bellomont gave his word and Kidd
walked headlong into the trap.

The moment he stepped ashore he was arrested, together

with his crew. His treasure, including the chests on Gardiner's Island, was seized, and since he could not be tried in the colonies he was shipped back to London. Here he languished for more than a year in Newgate Gaol. Two years had elapsed since his arrest. The Press, the Government and the public were howling for his blood. The Tories accused the Whigs and even the King of being in league with the famous pirate. None of his former friends dared to speak up in his defence.

Kidd stood trial on four separate occasions. There were six counts against him, five accusing him of piracy, one of murdering the gunner William Moore. The evidence was overwhelming and he was declared guilty on all indictments, the murder count being sufficient to send him to the gallows. On May 23rd, 1701, he was driven in an open cart to Execution Dock and hanged. The public, always to be relied upon to turn out in large numbers for such an occasion, got splendid entertainment for their money. The rope snapped and Kidd had to be strung up a second time. Later his body was taken to Tilbury and hung in chains in the customary fashion as an example to others.

So died the celebrated Captain Kidd, not perhaps as great as has often been claimed. Was he a pirate or a privateer? Did he receive a fair trial and deserve hanging? The questions will never be answered, nor, after all this time, does it greatly matter. But a couple of interesting facts have been pointed out by those who examined the case in some detail. The first relates to the evidence itself. The main witnesses for the prosecution, both on the murder and piracy charges, were Robert Bradinham and Joseph Palmer, both members of Kidd's crew. But both men admitted to having deserted him and both received a free pardon in return for their evidence, three days after Kidd was hanged.

The second point concerns two French passes. Passes were documents issued by governments to merchant ships to establish their identity and thus protect them against privateers. Kidd claimed that he took two such passes from the captains of the *Maiden* and *Quedagh Merchant*, indicating that the ships were French, not Armenian. This he sincerely believed. Since England and France were at war, these vessels were therefore legal prey. He said that he had handed over the passes to the Earl of Bellomont for safe keeping, and that Bellomont had guaranteed that they would help to clear his name. But by the time Kidd stood trial Bellomont was dead, and the passes were never produced in evidence. The court ruled that the whole story had been concocted and that the passes had never existed.

More than 200 years later, an American, hunting through the documents of the Public Records Office in London, discovered the two missing French passes. So perhaps Kidd, as he claimed repeatedly at his trial, was innocent after all.

15

Alexander Selkirk

The Real Robinson Crusoe

The example of Sir Henry Morgan soon spurred other English adventurers to chance their luck in the Pacific, the great ocean stretching westwards from the American continent to the shores of the East Indies and the Asian mainland. It was the Spanish and Portuguese navigators who had pioneered exploration in these waters, and it was only later that the seamen of Holland, England and France were to stake their claims to its island possessions. Sir Francis Drake had sailed across it but his had not been a voyage of discovery. All he had proved was that valuable plunder was to be had by raiding the towns and settlements on the west coast of South America and by lying in wait for the treasure galleons on their way up from Peru to Panama or across the ocean from the Philippines to Mexico. And the English buccaneers of the late seventeenth century did not try to conceal their motives. As one of their number wrote, ' 'Twas gold was the bait that tempted a pack of merry boys of us'.

These buccaneers – men such as Bartholomew Sharp, John Coxon, Richard Sawkins, John Cook, and Edward Davis – were not of the same calibre as Drake and Morgan. By and large they seem to have been an inefficient and quarrelsome lot. Their occasional successes in the South Sea were constantly being interrupted by desertions and mutinies, and it is hard to keep track of their expeditions, with frequent changes of command and grandiose plans yielding only meagre results. When they encountered setbacks in the Pacific they switched their attentions again to the Caribbean. But the good old days were gone, and piracy on the Spanish Main was no longer the sure road to fortune.

One English buccaneer who kept a fascinating record of his voyages, explored part of the coast of Northern Australia and sailed round the world three times, was William Dampier. He was intelligent, humane and an exceptionally experienced seaman. What is more, he was not simply interested in getting rich. In fact, he was not particularly successful as a pirate. He had served with John Coxon in a raid on Panama and in other expeditions to Spanish America, but was no better off than when he had started. Today he is better remembered, as he probably would have wished, as an author and explorer.

At one point in his career Dampier was associated with another remarkable pirate captain named Woodes Rogers. Here, too, was a man who had more vision and ambition than the run-of-the-mill type of fortune-seeking pirate. In fact, Rogers never admitted to being a pirate at all. He had a long career as a privateer and ended, like Henry Morgan, by hunting pirates on behalf of the Crown, as Governor of the Bahamas.

In 1708, Woodes Rogers, commanding the 320-ton frigate *Duke*, sailed on a privateering voyage to the South Sea. With him, as pilot, went William Dampier. They rounded Cape Horn in January 1709 and headed north. Many of the crew were suffering from scurvy, resulting from a diet which lacked fresh meat, fruit and vegetables, and Rogers decided to put in at the Spanish island of Juan Fernandez – supposed to be uninhabited – for recuperation and repairs. Dampier, who knew these waters well, identified the island without difficulty and a pinnace was lowered. But when the small rowing boat was some five miles from the shore, a wisp of smoke was seen curling up from trees behind the beach. The pinnace was hastily recalled, venturing out again the following day, this time with an officer and six men, all armed against a possible Spanish ambush.

The lookouts on the *Duke* watched tensely as the pinnace neared the shore. All was quiet. The sailors splashed

'Suddenly a grotesque figure appeared, stumbling
towards them'

through the surf and on to the beach. Suddenly a grotesque
figure appeared, stumbling towards them over the sand,
waving his arms wildly and uttering hoarse cries. He had
shaggy hair and a long beard and his ragged clothes were
made of goatskins. Apart from a knife hanging from his belt
he was unarmed. The amazed sailors kept him covered until
he was a few paces away. By then it was clear that he intended them no harm, for his gestures were friendly, not
threatening. Although his words were unclear they were able
to distinguish some English phrases, and soon they understood that he was pleading with them to take him back to
their ship.

The crew of the *Duke* watched with curiosity as the pinnace slowly made its way back with its strange occupant
aboard. But it was Dampier who recognized him, through
the rags and dirt, as a man who had once served with him on
a privateering voyage many years ago. And when the cast-
away in his turn saw the familiar face of Dampier, the
words began to tumble out and he began to relate an un-
believable story.

'My name,' he said, 'is Alexander Selkirk, and I was quartermaster aboard the galley *Cinque Ports*, commanded by
Captain Stradling.' This had been one of the ships which
had taken part in an expedition led by Dampier himself.
Selkirk was a Scot, with a stubborn nature and an inde-
pendent manner. He had clashed with Captain Stradling,
warning him that the *Cinque Ports* was unseaworthy, and
refused to sail any farther with him. Furious at such insol-
ence, Stradling offered him a choice. 'Either continue with
me, obeying my commands, or I leave you behind on Juan
Fernandez,' he threatened. Selkirk bravely chose to be put
ashore on the deserted island, perhaps in the belief that
friends would soon put in there and rescue him. He was allowed to take his personal possessions, including a Bible,
some books, tobacco and navigational instruments, as well
as a knife, hatchet, musket, powder and shot.

As it turned out, Selkirk's warning had been well justified.
The *Cinque Ports* eventually capsized and Stradling was

taken prisoner by the French. But Selkirk was hardly more fortunate. Nobody came to rescue him. No ship disturbed his solitude, and for four years and four months he was marooned on the island. Yet he managed to keep himself alive. He hunted goats to provide himself with food and clothing. He caught crawfish and found fresh water to drink. He built two huts and made his own furniture and cooking utensils. Previous visitors to the island had left behind hundreds of cats. These, together with some tame kids, were his sole companions and helped to get rid of the rats which also infested the island. As Woodes Rogers remarked admiringly in his journal, '. . . By the care of Providence and vigour of his youth, being now but about thirty years old, he came at last to conquer all the inconveniences of his solitude, and to be very easy'.

Both Woodes and Dampier were so impressed by Selkirk's enterprise and stamina in surviving his ordeal that they made him master of a Spanish galleon which they captured after rescuing him. It was two years before the expedition returned home and Selkirk immediately went back to his native village of Largo in Fife. But the long years of isolation seemed to have affected his mind. For some time he lived as a recluse in a cave in his father's garden. He eloped with a local girl, then married a widow. Finally he returned to the sea, dying on board the *Weymouth* in 1720.

After returning home Selkirk had briefly met the essayist Richard Steele, who was so fascinated by his tale that he wrote an account of it in one of his newspapers. Woodes Rogers had also published his version of the incident and the unusual story attracted the attention of the journalist and novelist Daniel Defoe. In 1719, he published a book which was based on the experiences of Alexander Selkirk. Its title was *The Life and Strange Surprising Adventures of Robinson Crusoe*.

16

Blackbeard

The Pirate who Was Larger than Life

Imagine a huge man, six feet four inches tall, broad and heavy, with a long black beard, twisted at the ends into tails, then tied with ribbons and looped over his ears. Under the brim of his black, three-cornered hat, this unruly giant was reported to stick matches which he would sometimes ignite. All this, combined with his flashing eyes, booming bass voice and generally wild and menacing appearance, gave him the look of a 'fury from Hell'. Such was one of the descriptions of Edward Teach, Tache or Thatch, better known, for obvious reasons, as Blackbeard. And many artists provided their own lurid impressions of this, one of the most feared of all the pirates of the Spanish Main.

Certainly, with his cutlass and three pairs of loaded pistols, Blackbeard must have been a formidable enemy. He was reputed to show no mercy to his victims, to have married fourteen wives who were made to dance for his pleasure while he shot at their feet, and who were walled up alive in his treasure vaults when he wanted to get rid of them.

He was the sort of character more likely to have been conjured out of dreams and nightmares, yet he really did exist. Born either in Bristol or the West Indies, and beginning his career at sea with a pirate captain named Benjamin Hornigold, he preyed on shipping off the North American coast for some two years, from 1716 until 1718. And that was just about the full extent of his career. Despite all the dramatic tales, he was not an especially daring pirate. Not only did he refuse to venture far from his bases in North

Carolina, but he hardly ever risked his life in open battle, preferring to attack lightly armed or defenceless vessels.

The pirates had seen their best days. Tew, Avery and Kidd were long dead. The Caribbean was relatively quiet, and even the pirates of the Red Sea and Indian Ocean were no longer a menace. The ports of New England derived little profit any more from pirates' loot. But there was still business to be done farther south in the seaboard states of North and South Carolina and Virginia. Blackbeard, if nothing else, was an astute businessman and there were plenty of dishonest merchants and people in high places who were prepared to help him to dispose of his contraband goods.

Blackbeard's flagship was the oddly named *Queen Anne's Revenge*, a captured French merchantman, mounting forty guns. His fleet was formidable enough to threaten to bring all local shipping to a standstill and more fearsome still after it had joined forces with the six ships of a certain Major Bonnet. Bonnet was a strange individual, an ex-planter who had taken to a pirate's life apparently because he could not endure his nagging wife! He had *bought* himself a sloop – something no pirate had ever done – recruited a crew and enjoyed some modest successes. Blackbeard met him off the Carolina coast and suggested a partnership. But there was never any doubt who was going to be the senior partner. Blackbeard considered Bonnet a mere amateur, relieved him of the captaincy of his own sloop and assigned him a minor role in their operations. Later he marooned seventeen of Bonnet's men, and they soon parted company! Bonnet went on his marauding way in his ship, the *Royal James*, was defeated in a battle with two Government sloops, tried, condemned to death, allowed to escape, recaptured and finally hanged.

Blackbeard's terrible reputation was now growing by leaps and bounds, though one suspects that he was not nearly as bad as his victims claimed. On one occasion, for example, he was blockading Charleston harbour and took a number of hostages, threatening to kill them if he were not immediately provided with certain medical supplies. Although several deadlines expired, Blackbeard did not carry out his threat and when the supplies were eventually handed over, sailed away peacefully enough – an incident which rather contradicts his reputation for rapacity and violence.

But there is one story about Blackbeard which is certainly true. He was drinking in his cabin with his mate and a gunner named Israel Hands. Suddenly he drew a pair of pistols, snuffed the candles and fired at random under the table. One bullet hit Hands in the knee and crippled him for life. It turned out to be a blessing in disguise, for although he ended up penniless in London, he was spared the gallows. And he acquired a measure of fame, too, when Robert Louis Stevenson used his name for the gunner on board the *Hispaniola* in *Treasure Island*.

The merchants and honest citizens of Charleston finally became so exasperated by the exploits of Blackbeard that they insisted on strong action being taken. The Governor of North Carolina declined to do so – he was in Blackbeard's pay and had personally married the pirate to a girl of fifteen, presumably the last of his numerous wives. So the Governor of Virginia took matters into his own hands. Blackbeard knew the risk he was running. King George I had recently offered a free pardon for any pirate who surrendered. Blackbeard had scornfully refused, so he had no reason to expect merciful treatment now if captured.

The Governor of Virginia's opportunity came when it was reported that Blackbeard had taken refuge, with a prize, in an inlet of the James River, part of Virginia territory. The inlet was too shallow to allow the passage of the two warships *Pearl* and *Lyme*, which had been sent to take the pirate. So the Governor bought two small sloops, placed them under the command of Lieutenant Robert Maynard, and sent them in, offering a reward of £100 for Blackbeard, dead or alive.

Maynard had no trouble sighting the pirate's nine-gun sloop, but as it was too dark to attack he decided to drop anchor for the night. Blackbeard had been warned but preferred to spend the night drinking with his men. Probably he felt confident of being able to negotiate the shallow waters, with their dangerous shoals and sandbanks, better than Maynard. At first light the following morning, seeing the two sloops blocking his exit, he steered for the beach and by drawing them after him managed to run them both aground. A broadside directed at the smaller sloop, as it lay helpless, shattered the mainmast and killed several of the crew.

It was a short-lived success. Maynard, an experienced seaman, tossed his anchor and heavy equipment overboard and worked his sloop off the sandbank. He then closed on Blackbeard, who, whilst frantically trying to hoist sail, had only managed to run his own sloop aground. Maynard prepared to board the enemy and called on Blackbeard to surrender. The deep voice of the pirate captain came booming back in defiance across the water.

Although cornered, Blackbeard was in a fighting mood. He downed a bowl of rum, drinking damnation to anyone who proposed asking or giving quarter. Now, with death and defeat staring him in the face, he put on a performance in the true, full-blooded pirate tradition. A well-aimed broadside struck Maynard's sloop, killing or wounding twenty of his men. In the billowing smoke, only Maynard and his helmsman could be seen. Blackbeard leapt on board, exhorting his crew to follow. It was a trap. As the pirates dashed towards the poop, thirty sailors attacked them from the rear and in a moment a fierce hand-to-hand battle was in progress. Outnumbered, the pirates were cornered. Nine of them were killed and the others handed over their weapons. Blackbeard alone showed real courage. Coming face to face with Maynard, he fired a pistol shot. It went wide, and Maynard's return shot wounded him slightly. Disregarding this, Blackbeard lunged at Maynard with his cutlass, the force of the blow breaking his opponent's sword. As the pirate hurled himself forward for the kill, a sailor slashed at his neck from behind and he fell to the deck. Although mortally wounded, he still fought off a dozen men surrounding him. Maynard fired again, yet still failed to finish him off. It was said that it

'Blackbeard lunged at Maynard with his cutlass'

took twenty-five separate gun shots or sword blows to kill him.

To prove that the famous pirate was really dead, Maynard cut off his head and hung it on the end of his bowsprit. He had earned his £100. The surviving members of Blackbeard's crew were tried and hanged. As for their captain, few mourned his passing. Captain Charles Johnson, who told his story in *A General History of the Pirates*, summed it up succinctly. 'Here was an end,' he wrote, 'of that courageous brute, who might have passed in the world for a hero had he been employed in a good cause.'

17

James Plantain

The African Pirate King

Avery, Kidd and many other renowned pirates barely lived long enough to enjoy the fruits of their successes. Their careers were fiery and brief, like the passage of meteors through a night sky. Yet some of their less famous colleagues, by a combination of shrewdness and good fortune, managed to escape both the hangman's noose and the pauper's grave, and indeed to spend much of their lives in luxurious retirement. And there are few stranger stories than that of a Jamaican-born pirate named James Plantain, the King of Ranter Bay.

Little is known of Plantain's early exploits except that he made a fortune from piracy both in the Atlantic and the Arabian Sea. The really fascinating part of his story begins with his arrival, around the year 1720, on the island of Madagascar, off the south-east coast of Africa, a popular pirate haunt. The country evidently appealed to him so much that he decided to settle there. When, two years later, Commodore Thomas Matthews, the pirate hunter, anchored off the coast with three naval vessels to hunt for Plantain, he was astonished to be greeted by a well-dressed white man, who introduced himself as 'James Plantain, ex-pirate' and now a local ruler.

The King of Ranter Bay, as he called himself, owned a large tract of territory in the southern tip of the island. He lived in a large, fortress-type house with a bevy of wives to whom he had given such exotic English names as Moll, Kate, Sue and Pegg, and he commanded a small but loyal army of native soldiers. From the manner in which his wives were dressed – fine Indian silks and diamond necklaces – Matthews concluded that Plantain had turned his fortune to good advantage; and there was still sufficient money to pay for the clothing and wine that Matthews was only too happy to sell. If he had any thoughts of arresting Plantain as a pirate, he very soon decided that it would be more prudent to make an ally of this powerful local king. Clearly his army was more than a match for his own naval contingent, and well commanded too; for Plantain had with him two other experienced former pirates, a young Scotsman named James Adair and a Dane, Hans Burgen. So Matthews sailed away from Madagascar, his mission incomplete, leaving the King of Ranter Bay to his own devices.

Plantain, however, was not satisfied with his limited empire. The island was at that time broken up into a number of small kingdoms and Plantain had already clashed with some of his neighbours, striking deep into their territory, stealing their cattle and exacting tribute from them. One such neighbour, on the west coast, nicknamed King Dick by the pirates, had a possession that Plantain particularly coveted, a grand-daughter named Eleanora Brown, a beautiful half-caste girl who was rumoured to be the daughter of a Bristol sea captain. Plantain decided that a girl with a European background and breeding would lend dignity to his harem, and requested King Dick's permission to marry her. When her grandfather refused, Plantain sent a strong native force, armed with lances and rifles, against him. Commanding his army was a tall, handsome man named Mulatto Tom. He described himself as the son of the notorious Captain Avery and the daughter of the Great Mogul, and there was nobody to disprove this somewhat extravagant claim. With him marched the armies of several other local kings, including one popularly known as King Kelly.

The King of Ranter Bay advanced on three fronts, with English, Scottish and Danish flags flying, and soon defeated King Dick's motley army, which included a number of English pirates. Two of these men were promptly tortured to death and King Dick was captured. All might then have ended in concord and friendship had not Plantain discovered that the Princess Eleanora was due to have a baby and that the father had been one of the English pirates killed in the battle. By a strange transfer of blame, Plantain proceeded to execute her unfortunate grandfather and to burn his capital to the ground. Then for good measure he set fire to King Kelly's capital of Mannagore as well.

The lovely Eleanora, who after all was the real culprit, escaped punishment. She became Plantain's favourite wife, with the name of Nelly. He was delighted to discover that she knew the rudiments of the Christian faith, so he continued her education and permitted her to become the mother of several children. He guarded her jealously too, for when another English pirate was discovered trying to make love to her, he was executed on the spot.

But power must have gone to James Plantain's head, for now he decided that he was strong enough to make a bid to become King of Madagascar entire. In a series of wars, culminating in the capture of Fort Dauphin and the deaths of the local monarch and the fugitive King Kelly, Plantain, for a brief spell, achieved his ambition. Back at Ranter Bay he entertained his loyal subjects, as well as the English, French and Dutch settlers of Madagascar, on a lavish scale.

Yet it was just too good to last. He had made too many enemies and was only able to maintain his power by cruelly oppressing his subjects. With rebellion in the offing, he built himself a sloop, and taking only Eleanora and her children with him, sailed to the Malabar Coast. Here he was welcomed and possibly entered the service of the pirate Angria. And that is the last that history records of James Plantain, the first and probably the only pirate king.

18

Mary Read and Anne Bonny

Tigresses of the Caribbean

In November 1728, a Jamaican court sentenced a group of pirates to the gallows. When asked whether they had anything to say before they were hanged, two of them caused a sensation by announcing to the judge: 'My lord, we plead our bellies!' Amid scenes of consternation it was then discovered that the two pirates were, in fact, women. Both of them were found to be pregnant and according to law were spared the death penalty!

The names of these women were Mary Read and Anne Bonny. They had lived and fought as pirates in the Caribbean for many years, sharing the dangers and privations of shipboard life and, by all accounts, acting in as brave and bloodthirsty a manner as their male comrades.

They were not the first female pirates in history. In medieval times, for example, there was a Gothic princess named Alwilda who became the captain of a pirate vessel in the Baltic. Later, during the reign of Queen Elizabeth I, the mother of Sir John Killigrew, who combined the post of Vice-Admiral of Cornwall with a flourishing trade in piracy, won an international reputation on her own account. She was herself the daughter of a 'gentleman-pirate' and together with her son controlled a powerful pirate syndicate. The Killigrew house at Falmouth had a secret passage leading down to the shore and Lady Killigrew entertained many of the leading pirates of the age. Yet hers was not merely a domestic and passive role. On a January night in 1582 she led a band of armed servants aboard a German ship which was lying at anchor in Falmouth harbour. The unsuspecting crew members were killed and their bodies tossed over the side. Then her servants carried back to the house several bolts of cloth and two barrels full of pieces of eight. As a result Lady Killigrew was arrested, tried and sentenced to death. But although her two servants were executed, she received a last-minute reprieve.

Mary Read and Anne Bonny, more than a century later, could not boast such distinguished backgrounds. Anne was probably born in Ireland. The illegitimate daughter of a lawyer, she lived for a time with her father in South Carolina, had numerous love affairs, was deserted by her husband and finally made her way to the port of Charleston. Here she met the dashing pirate captain, John Rackham, nicknamed Calico Jack because of his striped calico shirt and trousers. Rackham had once been a member of Captain Avery's pirate crew and was now a wanted man, having turned down the offer of a free pardon. Anne fell in love with the handsome, impetuous pirate and joined him on board his ship, disguising herself as a man. Although Rackham did not give her away, it seems unlikely that in such a closed community she was able to conceal her identity for very long. But once she had proved that she was as tough in manner and speech as any of the pirates, she was accepted by them as an equal.

Of course, there were bound to be complications. Anne soon discovered that she was going to have a baby, and Rackham was obliged to put her ashore with friends in Cuba. Once the baby was born, however, and farmed out to foster-parents, Anne was back at sea with her lover, helping him to scour the Caribbean for prizes and flourishing her cutlass alongside her shipmates. One day they took a Dutch vessel bound for the West Indies and signed on most of the crew. Anne Bonny's roving eye fastened upon one burly young man, so she took him aside and revealed to him that she was not like the other pirates on board. The ensuing scene has to be left to the imagination. For, to her dismay and astonishment, the young 'man' who had attracted her also had a secret to disclose. He, too, was a woman in disguise, by the name of Mary Read! Once all the confusion was cleared up, the two girls became close friends.

Mary's parents were English and her early history was even more colourful and improbable than Anne's. Her mother had wanted to have the child supported financially by her mother-in-law. For some reason the old lady was prejudiced against girls, so, in order to deceive her, Mary had to be dressed up and reared as a boy. This disguise apparently suited Mary so well that she decided to retain it long into her teens. She went to sea, serving on a man-of-war, then deserted and signed up with the English Army in Flanders. But, as happened with Anne Bonny, romance intervened. She fell in love with a Dutch soldier in the same regiment and married him. When he died, she again cut her hair short, put on her man's clothes and slipped on board a ship bound for the Indies. On the way out it was captured by Calico Jack and Mary found herself a pirate.

The pirate life suited Mary's adventurous nature admirably and she, too, won the respect of her comrades for her courage and fighting ability. But she could not conceal the softer side of her nature. During one expedition Rackham took a number of Jamaican vessels and recruited some craftsmen. Mary fell deeply in love with one young man but was unable to disclose her true feelings. The lad was pleasant and good looking but not much of a fighter, and for that reason was teased unmercifully by the crew. One day he could endure their taunts no longer and rashly challenged one of the ringleaders to a duel. According to the Pirates' Articles, this was arranged to take place on shore the following day, with the captain himself presiding.

Mary knew that the young man would probably be killed so she resolved to take his place. At dawn the next day she picked a quarrel with the same ruffian, who, like everybody else, took her to be a man, and provoked him into challenging her to a duel. She made certain that it would take place a couple of hours before the other. Anne Bonny and Calico Jack were the only persons who shared her secret and he must have been sorely tempted to call the whole thing off. He need not have worried. On the order to fire, two pistol shots rang out. It was Mary's opponent who fell wounded to the sand, and Mary's cutlass that whipped down to deal the death blow.

It would be pleasant to record a happy ending to the story. Mary, it is true, married her young man, but their joy was not to last long. Calico Jack's ship was boarded and captured by a Government sloop in a remote island hideout. Rackham himself put up a miserable performance for he was drunk with most of the crew, and the guns were not even loaded. In fact, it was Mary Read and Anne Bonny, who were the last members of the crew to resist capture, lashing out furiously with their cutlasses and heaping abuse on their cowardly shipmates. But it was hopeless. Calico Jack and his crew were handed over to justice and soon Mary found herself standing beside her husband in the dock, together with Rackham and Anne Bonny.

Calico Jack behaved with as little gallantry in court as he had shown bravery in action. He betrayed all his friends and appeared as a prosecution witness against Mary Read. Little wonder then at Anne Bonny's last message to him when she visited him on the eve of his execution. 'I am sorry,' she said, 'to see you there, but if you had fought like a man, you need not have been hanged like a dog.' Anne herself was reprieved and served a gaol sentence. What happened to her when she was released is not known. Her friend Mary Read was certainly less fortunate. Her husband was duly hanged and she herself died shortly afterwards from a fever caught while in prison.

19

Bartholomew Roberts

The Last of the Great Pirates

'No gaming at cards or dice for money; no women permitted; no fighting allowed; lights and candles to be put out at eight o'clock.' It sounds more like regulations for a boarding school than rules for a pirate vessel. And these are only a few of the Articles laid down by Captain Bartholomew Roberts, the last of the great pirates.

Roberts was indeed a strict disciplinarian, more so than most pirate captains. This was partly as a result of his Welsh religious upbringing, but it was partly plain common-sense. All pirate crews were bound to observe certain rules for their own safety and protection. But on Roberts' ships, which bore such optimistic names as *Fortune, Good Fortune* and *Royal Fortune*, the rules were tempered by a genuine consideration for the welfare both of crew members and prisoners. Roberts was undoubtedly a dedicated pirate and a successful one. He was reckoned to have taken over 400 ships during his career, easily a record, and the man who eventually brought his exploits to a close received a knighthood for it. But he was no rum-swigging, foul-mouthed, uneducated ruffian. He drank no hard liquor himself, yet he was no prude. He recognized that his men needed relaxation and that they were only human. His own weakness, and it was not a very serious one, was a craving for fine clothes. With a single exception, he was never found guilty of an outrageous act of cruelty, he was intelligent, a first-class seaman and so popular with his crew that many of them wept when he was killed in action.

Bartholomew Roberts

Born in Pembrokeshire, Bartholomew Roberts started life on the right side of the law as master of a slave ship. When it was captured in 1719 by another Welsh pirate named Howel Davis, Roberts had little choice but to join him and so he too became a pirate. Davis was killed by enemy action only six weeks later and Roberts, although a new recruit, was popularly elected to replace him as captain. There were a few dissenters among the senior officers, who were in the habit of strutting around calling themselves 'Lords'. One of them was heard to grumble, 'I do not care who you choose as captain so long as it is not a Papist'. On such grounds Roberts was certainly acceptable and the others openly admitted that they had selected him as 'a man of courage and skilled in navigation, one who by his council and bravery seems best able to defend the Commonwealth and ward us from the dangers and tempests of an unstable element, and the fatal consequence of anarchy'. High-sounding words indeed, but Roberts fully repaid their trust. Confidently accepting their decision, Roberts replied, 'Since I have dipped my hands in muddy water and must be a pirate, I would far rather be a commander than a common man'.

The new captain soon showed his mettle by taking revenge on the Portuguese who had been responsible for Davis' death. He captured two of their ships and then sailed his 32-gun vessel *Royal Rover* clear across the South Atlantic to Brazil. Here he carried out one of the boldest raids in the history of piracy. In the Bay of Bahia he came across forty-two large vessels, part of the Portuguese Treasure Fleet, about to sail for Lisbon. Hardly pausing to consider the tremendous odds against him, Roberts sailed boldly into their midst, anchoring alongside one of the ships. He greeted the Portuguese captain in a friendly manner and calmly informed him that he need have nothing to fear if only he would point out to him the richest ship in the fleet. Taken completely aback, the captain indicated a 40-gun vessel named the *Sagrada Familia*. Roberts set course for her but the ruse was discovered, the alarm was given and the guns manned. But he got in a broadside and before the Portuguese could recover their wits his men had boarded her. Then, with the loss of only two men and using his own ship for cover, Roberts sailed the *Sagrada Familia* out into the open sea. She was found to be carrying sugar, skins and tobacco to a considerable value and, better still, 40,000 gold moidores – roughly £50,000.

They shared out the booty on Devil's Island, off the coast of Guiana, lived happily for a few weeks on the proceeds and captured a sloop which they renamed *Good Fortune*. In his new ship, Roberts wrought havoc with West Indian shipping and while the authorities were vainly searching for him, appeared unexpectedly far to the north, off the coast of Newfoundland. Here he busied himself plundering English and French trawlers and fishing villages, then entered the port of Trepanny, ransacking it without resistance and capturing upwards of twenty ships. Once again he was greatly outnumbered but on this occasion he made no attempt to conceal his intentions. Indeed, he is said to have used a form of psychological warfare, sailing in with all his musicians on deck, blowing trumpets, ringing bells and beating drums. They made such a din that their opponents were usually too petrified to fight back. Alongside the English flag at the masthead was his private emblem of a death's head and cutlass.

This daring exploit earned the grudging admiration even of the authorities who were determined to capture him. Roberts made no attempt to lie low, increasing the size of his fleet by capturing a number of French vessels, keeping one 26-gunner for himself and renaming it the *Royal Fortune*. Then he continued his escapades in the West Indies. At about that time he changed his flag as a result of unfriendly treatment received at the hands of the Governors of Barbados and Martinique. The new ensign showed himself astride two skulls, one bearing the initials ABH (A Barbadian's Head) and the other AMH (A Martiniquian's Head). It spoke for itself. From then on he showed no mercy to any prisoner unfortunate enough to have been born in either of these islands.

Soon he was back across the Atlantic and off the Guinea coast. His return to African waters was not because of any pressure exerted on him by his enemies but simply because there was hardly any shipping worth mentioning left in the Caribbean. His long run of successes continued without interruption. Very rarely did a ship pluck up enough courage to offer serious resistance. And whenever a prize fell into his hands, Roberts stuck to his principle of never forcing a prisoner to sign with him. Once he found a clergyman among the personnel of a captured vessel. Roberts politely invited him to join his ship as chaplain, but the parson firmly refused. So Roberts let him go, keeping for his own use the parson's three prayer books and corkscrew!

Eventually, of course, he sailed into trouble. Two British men-of-war were now patrolling the African coast and protecting local shipping. In February 1722, Roberts cruised along the coast, unaware that the patrol ships had sighted him and were preparing to attack. When the leading British ship, the *Swallow*, appeared on the horizon, Roberts mistook her for a Portuguese merchantman and sent one of his own vessels, the *Great Ranger*, to pursue her. The *Swallow* pretended to turn tail, then suddenly rounded on the pirate ship and, after a sharp exchange of fire, captured her.

On the morning of February 10th, the *Swallow* came upon the *Royal Fortune* at anchor and closed in for the kill. As luck would have it, most of Roberts' crew were drunk – in defiance of his regulations – and Roberts himself was at breakfast. When he managed to muster the crew to repel the imminent attack by the man-of-war it was already too late. In the very first exchange of broadsides Roberts was struck by a volley of grape shot and fell to the deck, killed instantly. His men continued fighting for a while, though with their captain dead they had little heart left. But before they surrendered they buried him, as he had instructed, by lowering his body over the side of the ship. He was dressed in his full regalia, as was his custom, in a 'rich crimson damask waistcoat and breeches, a red feather in his hat, a gold chain round his neck, with a diamond cross hanging to it, a sword in his hand and two pairs of pistols, hanging at the end of a silk sling'. A bold and colourful figure he must have cut indeed in this, his final action.

Of the 169 men who were captured and placed on trial, fifty-two were publicly hanged, a humiliation which was spared their captain. But with the death of Captain Bartholomew Roberts, the great age of piracy drew to its close.

20

The Angrias

Terrors of the Malabar Coast

If the two Barbarossas were the terrors of the Mediterranean in the sixteenth century, the two Angrias earned an equally evil reputation 200 years later off the Malabar Coast of India – not brothers this time but father and son.

Kanhoji Angria, the father, was originally the Admiral of the Mahratta Navy, an Indian fleet detailed to preserve law and order along the Malabar Coast. As so often happens, power went to his head and he had soon thrown off all authority in order to build up a fleet of his own. With these ships he was soon able to carry out audacious pirate raids on other vessels, especially on the ships of the important East India Company. And to support and reinforce his fleet he constructed fortresses at strategic points along the Coast. When the Company protested he retorted, 'I claim the right to seize your ships whenever I can!'

He carried out his threat only too thoroughly, eventually fortifying an island at the very entrance to the port of Bombay, from which vantage point he menaced every ship coming in and out of the busy harbour. Once he captured an armed vessel belonging to the Governor of Bombay himself. Two English passengers were taken prisoner, together with all the ship's officers, and all ransomed for 30,000 rupees (about £3,000).

The Company made half-hearted efforts to cut Kanhoji down to size, but his supremacy was not really threatened until a new Governor of Bombay came out in 1715. The Governor bolstered the defences of the city and formed a fleet of frigates and other vessels to challenge Kanhoji. Unfortunately, his officers were far less competent and enthusiastic than the Governor himself, so that little impact was made in the skirmishes that followed. Messages were sent to England for reinforcements, and the celebrated Commodore Matthews (the same man who had been royally entertained by the King of Ranter Bay) spent two years in Indian waters without once capturing a pirate. His idea had been to form a local alliance with the Portuguese so that they could defeat the pirates together. But during the first joint attack on one of Kanhoji's strongholds, the Portuguese turned tail and fled. Matthews, in his fury, struck the Portuguese commander across the face with his cane, and that was the end of the brief partnership. The Governor returned home, bitterly disappointed, and Kanhoji delivered a parting memento by attacking his three ships on the way.

Seven years later Kanhoji died, leaving five sons to dispute the succession. For ten years they did exactly that, and the Angria fortunes swayed first in favour of one brother, then another. The British and Portuguese never knew which of them to attack. Eventually an illegitimate son named Tulaji outwitted his half-brothers and became undisputed master of the Angria empire. He first gave warning that a new and even more formidable menace than Kanhoji was loose in the area when he attacked an East India Company convoy, protected by two warships. After a fierce battle, Tulaji sailed off with five English vessels as prizes. Some years later he boarded and captured the Bombay Marine's strongest ship, the *Restoration*. The English gunnery on this occasion was so pathetic that although the battle lasted many hours the pirate ships were almost undamaged; and when they boarded her, the incompetent crew offered no resistance.

Tulaji's vessels preyed on English, Portuguese, and Dutch shipping along the length of the Malabar Coast, not at all daunted by four warships sent to Bombay expressly to protect cargo ships in convoy. There was generally a straggler to be picked up if the pirates waited patiently. Much more

effective was the East India Company's campaign to destroy
the Angria land forts. Commodore William James, in the
40-gun *Protector*, led a squadron in attacking the chief
pirate base at Severndroog in March 1755.

The pirate fleet sailed out to meet James' ships but disappeared over the horizon after showing surprisingly little
desire to fight. James was now able to concentrate his fire on
the fortress of Severndroog, which stood at the tip of a rocky
peninsula, protected by three smaller forts on the landward
side. The sea bombardment lasted all day. That night, a des-
erter from the fort disclosed that many men had been killed
and that much damage had been done. Next day the *Protector* engaged all four forts at once, the upper-deck guns
and small arms being directed at Severndroog, the lower-
deck guns, with those from two bomb ketches, taking on the
smaller forts. Shortly after midday a magazine exploded on
Severndroog, and the survivors were seen making for the
mainland in their boats. By the following morning all the
forts had surrendered.

This was a severe blow to Tulaji and it encouraged the
Government to attempt a similar onslaught on the equally
well-defended stronghold of Gheriah the following year. The
Company sent eighteen ships, again commanded by
Commodore James, carrying 214 guns, to which were added
six naval vessels. A force of 800 Europeans and 600 natives
stood by for landing. They were led by a lieutenant-colonel
named Robert Clive, later to become the famous soldier and
statesman known as Clive of India.

Against this strong force Tulaji had paraded a fleet of
fifty-eight warships, including the captured *Restoration*. He
knew that the expedition's instructions were to take him
dead or alive. The Bombay Council had been very explicit on
how to deal with him:

'It is probable that Tulaji Angria may offer to capitulate,
and possibly offer a sum of money, but you are to consider
that this fellow is not on a footing with any prince in the
known world, he being a pirate in whom no confidence can
be put, not only taking, burning, and destroying ships of all

nations, but even the vessels belonging to the natives, which have his own passes, and for which he has annually collected large sums of money. Should he offer any sum of money it must be a very great one that will pay us for the many rich ships he has taken (which we cannot enumerate), besides the innumerable other smaller vessels.'

More than 150 guns poured a deadly barrage of fire on the pirate fleet which was drawn up across the mouth of the river defending the fort. Against this merciless bombardment the pirates had no effective reply. Within two hours almost every ship was on fire, and the blaze soon spread to buildings on shore. With Angria's fleet destroyed, Clive's troops landed unopposed, digging in about a mile and a half from the fortress, which was now pounded from land and sea.

A flag of truce was sent in but the defenders refused to surrender. Then the four huge line-of-battle ships joined in the bombardment. Suddenly a tremendous explosion shook the fort, and shortly afterwards the white flag was seen fluttering from its tower. Clive's men took booty to the value of £130,000 in gold, silver, and jewels, dividing it among themselves and the naval forces. Tulaji, who had personally conducted the defence, prudently surrendered, not to the English, but to the native Mahratta troops. It made little difference. The last of the Angria family languished in prison for the rest of his life, and the power of the Malabar pirates was ended for ever.

21

Mrs Ching

Queen of the China Seas

Even as late as the beginning of the nineteenth century the
China Seas were still controlled by pirates, and none of them
was more powerful than Ching Yih. His immense fleet of
war junks, manned by 70,000 men, was divided into six
squadrons. Each squadron carried its own colour – red,
yellow, blue, green, black, and white. The senior red squadron was under the personal command of the pirate chief's
wife, Ching Yih Saou. When her husband was drowned in a
storm in 1807 she assumed overall command of his fleet.

Mrs Ching, as she was popularly known, proved to be as
bold and resourceful a pirate as her late husband, holding
the powerful Chinese Navy at bay for many years. At the
peak of her power she controlled the movements of several
thousand war junks. These were unwieldy vessels with high
sterns and low bows, bamboo-matting sails rigged to two or
three masts, and normally mounted with up to fifteen guns.
Mrs Ching's own flagship was considerably larger, however,
with thirty-eight guns, two of them 24-pounders, the others
6- and 12-pounders. Although well armed, the junks were
slow-moving vessels, and the crew (frequently accompanied
by wives and children) were crammed tightly together in un-
hygienic quarters below decks. The ships were overrun by
vermin (rats were often eaten – so too, if we are to believe one
English prisoner, was a dish of boiled rice and caterpillars)
and reeked of unwashed bodies and opium fumes. Such then
were the ships which Mrs Ching and her captains led to do

battle with English and Portuguese shipping in the China Seas.

Mrs Ching was a stern and capable commander. To succeed her as commander of the red squadron, she appointed her lieutenant and lover, Chang Paoa. Her other officers assumed picturesque names such as 'Scourge of the Eastern Sea', 'Frogs' Meal', and 'Jewel of the Whole Crew'. The Articles which governed the crews' behaviour aboard her ships were similar to those of the early buccaneers of the Spanish Main, but if anything more severe. For example, if a crew member went ashore without permission he was likely to have his ears split in public; if he repeated the offence, he was liable to be put to death. Plunder from any captured ships was to be properly registered and only one-fifth divided among the pirates; the rest was set aside in a general fund, and if any pirate was caught stealing from this fund, he was executed. Women captives were to be protected and if any man was found guilty of violating a prisoner he would also be put to death. Desertion and cowardice, as on all pirate vessels, were similarly punished. It was indeed a hard life. Nor, if he were captured by the authorities, could a pirate expect anything less painful. In all probability he would be beheaded and his head set out for public show. Little wonder if he preferred to endure the discomfort and harsh discipline of Mrs Ching's junks. At least they held out the hope of excitement and profit.

Much of Mrs Ching's success was due to her skill as a business woman and the friendly relations she enjoyed with farmers and villagers who kept her fleet provided with rice and wine. By doing so they were risking their lives, for the Government threatened to execute anyone found guilty of supplying provisions to the pirates and to flog or transport anyone who bought stolen goods from them.

In 1808, a great battle was fought between Mrs Ching's pirate fleet and a Government naval squadron. Together with Chang Paoa she prepared an ambush, concealing the main part of her fleet behind a headland and sending out

only a couple of decoy ships. The Chinese admiral fell headlong into the trap and was soon completely surrounded by
the pirate war junks. Just the same, he fought bravely from
dawn to dusk, until the sea's surface was littered with the
bodies of dead sailors and pirates. Sixteen Government
junks were taken and three more sunk. The admiral, looking
for an honourable death, taunted Chang Paoa with insults.
But the pirate, impressed by the old man's bravery, refused
to be provoked and spoke kindly to him. The admiral, re-
fusing the humiliation of capture, then committed suicide.

Next year another Government fleet set sail to destroy
Mrs Ching's pirates. This time it was commanded by an
inexperienced general who tried to run away as soon as he
spotted the enemy fleet. But he was prevented from doing so
when the wind suddenly dropped and becalmed his ships.
All the pirates had to do was to swim across the placid
waters and clamber on board the rival vessels, where a general massacre promptly ensued.

The tide turned for a while when yet another admiral, with
100 junks, inflicted heavy damage on the pirates by ordering
his gunners to fire first at the bamboo-matting sails of the
pirate junks and then at their steering gear, so as to immo-
bilize them. As the flames spread rapidly, the pirates panicked and took to the oars. One pirate's wife defended her
junk bravely, slashing at her enemies with a cutlass in either
hand until she was wounded and taken prisoner. But in the
face of disaster, Mrs Ching rallied her crews and fought
back. Bringing up two more squadrons as reinforcements,
she surrounded the enemy fleet and scattered it.

This formidable woman seemed quite invincible. Her next
victim was Admiral Ting-kwei, who found himself trapped
in harbour by a fleet of 200 pirate junks. His officers,
alarmed at the overwhelming odds facing them, at first refused to fight, but the admiral delivered a rousing speech
and the battle that followed was a furious one. Within a few
minutes 'Jewel of the Whole Crew' had been killed by a
cannon ball and things looked black for the pirates. But
Chang Paoa appeared in the nick of time, singled out the

admiral's flagship and encircled it with his junks. Realizing that all was lost, Ting-kwei in his turn committed suicide and all his ships surrendered.

Mrs Ching had now completely established her supremacy and the Chinese Government wisely made no further attempt to challenge her on the open seas. Her junks plundered villages and shipping up and down the coasts, even sailing unopposed up the rivers, burning towns, and taking thousands of prisoners. One village which put up an unexpectedly stout resistance was so thoroughly plundered and devastated that it was said later, 'You could not hear the cry of a dog or a hen'.

Mrs Ching's eventual downfall came about not as a result of her own strategic shortcomings, but through certain womanly weaknesses. The commander of the black squadron, O-po-tae, was intensely jealous of Chang Paoa and his special relationship with Mrs Ching. The two men quarrelled violently on a number of occasions and soon their squadrons were at war with each other. Chang's ships were badly mauled; he lost sixteen junks and 300 sailors. This break in the pirate ranks sparked off more trouble in other sections of the fleet. In the end, O-po-tae deserted to the Emperor with his 160 armed junks and 8,000 men. Chang Paoa recovered from his defeat and continued his marauding privately, but Mrs Ching was by this time so completely disillusioned that she too decided to strike a bargain with the Emperor. Rather surprisingly, she was pardoned, together with her crews. Encouraged by her mild treatment, Chang Paoa followed her example, was given the rank of major and turned to pirate chasing. Shortly afterwards the green and yellow pirate squadrons also surrendered and the menace of organized piracy was ended for about thirty years. It was said that Mrs Ching turned her considerable talents to smuggling and that she lived comfortably for many years – one person who could reasonably claim that 'crime does pay'.

22

Jean and Pierre Lafitte

The Overlords of New Orleans

The careers of many pirates are full of gaps. Usually, very little is known of their relatively innocent early years. Often the true facts about their death are never known. In the case of the Lafitte brothers there are question marks at both ends. Not only do we not know where they came from but we have no reliable information as to how and where they ended their lives. But they certainly made an indelible mark on the history of the colourful American city of New Orleans in the early part of the nineteenth century.

There were two brothers, Jean and Pierre. Judging by their names they were of French origin, but there were many families in New Orleans and the state of Louisiana with French backgrounds. At one time they were blacksmiths, but later they turned their wits to smuggling and piracy, or to give it a politer term, privateering.

It was, undoubtedly, Jean, the elder brother, who dictated policy. His name crops up far more frequently in the history books. But both of them made their headquarters on an island in Barataria Bay, down river from the port of New Orleans. The locals were tough and none too law-abiding, and provided many willing recruits for the Lafittes' pirate ships. They carried out daring raids all along the coast and down into the Gulf of Mexico, selling their loot profitably in New Orleans and other towns. They even resold slaves destined for the West Indies to the cotton planters of Louisiana, charging by weight, a dollar a pound – not a bad business deal.

'They resold slaves destined for the West Indies'

Soon they were flaunting their newly found wealth in the streets of New Orleans. They wore the most expensive clothes, dined in the best restaurants, and were seen regularly in the local theatre. Once, the Governor, acting reluctantly after complaints from local merchants and ship-owners, had them arrested on a charge of piracy. The brothers simply hired the best lawyers in town and walked out of the courtroom, free men.

In 1812, America was once more at war with Britain. From their base in Barataria Bay, the Lafitte brothers commanded the approaches to New Orleans, a vital port which the British aimed to capture. Taking advantage of the Lafittes' temporary difficulties with the Governor, the British approached them and offered them 30,000 dollars and commissions in the Royal Navy. The brothers stalled, then went straight to the American commander, General Andrew Jackson, and tendered him their services. Pirates they might be, but traitors they were not. Thanks to the efforts of the Lafitte pirate crews, who were especially effective in the artillery units, the Americans won a resounding victory in the battle of New Orleans in 1815. The British lost almost 2,000 men, the Americans only thirteen.

After the war, although they were both granted free pardons, the Lafittes considered it safer to get away from their old hunting grounds, and moved their headquarters to an island which later became the site of the city of Galveston in Texas. Here they continued their privateering exploits against the Spanish, wielding immense power locally and outwitting every attempt to catch them. But as the years passed, the Government exerted stronger pressure, especially after one of their attacks on some American vessels. There is no further trace of Pierre, but Jean is said to have sailed away to an undisclosed destination in his favourite ship *The Pride*. One report said that he was eventually killed with sixty of his crew in a battle against a British sloop. There are other versions of his death, all contradictory and doubtless legendary. The Lafittes succeeded in providing mystery right to the end.

23

The Red Army

Skyjackers over Japan

The old-time pirates, with their black flags, bloodstained cutlasses, and treasure chests, have long since disappeared. Yet piracy is not dead, even in our twentieth century. In recent years it has taken on a new and alarmingly dangerous form. The pirates have taken to the air, and their victims are the crews and passengers of international airlines.

The normal 'hijacking' or 'skyjacking' procedure calls for the air pirates to mingle with the passengers and make their identities known at some stage during the flight. They then force the captain to fly the aeroplane to a different destination – usually to Cuba or the Middle East. The danger of a bullet or grenade shattering the fuselage and bringing disaster to everyone on board generally gives the captain no alternative. Some airlines now regularly carry armed guards to foil hijacking attempts, but this is a risky and expensive business. Occasionally the hijacker is disarmed or even killed, but more often the captain agrees to fly to a new destination. There the passengers are usually freed and the airliner returned to its owners.

Often the hijacker works alone. Sometimes he is clearly mentally deranged, as was the case with the young American who demanded a ransom of millions of dollars, only to be duped with a pile of empty mail bags and eventually overpowered. The risk of tackling a madman in mid-air carries obvious risks, but more serious still is the threat to the lives of innocent people posed by organized gangs of hijackers who are acting for political reasons. Two such hijackings hit the headlines in 1970. The first involved a Japanese airliner and a group of fanatical, sword-waving students. The second occurred in the Middle East and triggered off an international crisis.

On the morning of March 31st, 1970, a Boeing 727 belonging to Japan Airlines took off from Tokyo airport on a routine domestic flight to Fukuoka, on the island of Kyushu, a distance normally covered in about one hour. On board, in addition to a crew of nine, were 129 passengers, some of them women. All, except for two Americans, were Japanese.

The passengers had just released their seat belts and were settling down to their magazines and newspapers when a group of young men suddenly leapt to their feet. To the alarm and amazement of the passengers they began to flourish samurai-type swords, rushing up the aisle towards the flight deck and pushing the stewardesses roughly in front of them. It occurred to one or two of the passengers that they were making some kind of film, but it soon became quite clear that something far more serious and perilous was afoot. The first the captain knew of anything being wrong was when he felt the point of a sword against his throat. Alarmed, he found himself staring into the blazing eyes of a young man who barked out a command. 'Don't move, or I cut your throat! Turn the plane round at once and fly us to North Korea!'

Captain Ishida kept cool. Realizing that if he made a false move he could be responsible for the deaths of everyone on board, he sent a radio message to ground control. 'I am being hijacked,' he reported. 'I have been directed to fly to Pyongyang in North Korea.' But already his mind was busy with alternatives. He pointed out to the hijacker that the plane was not carrying enough fuel to make the longer flight to North Korea and that it would be necessary to land, as planned, in Fukuoka. Reluctantly, the hijacker gave his permission but issued a grim warning that he and his friends would be on their guard against any traps or deliberate delays.

In the meantime, the other hijackers patrolled the aisles, swords and daggers drawn, forcing the terrified passengers to stay in their seats. Some of the men protested and quickly found themselves with their hands tied behind their backs. One passenger was hit over the head with a pistol butt. None of the others were in any way harmed. The young men explained that they belonged to an extreme Communist organization of students known as the Red Army. Although they remained perfectly courteous and chatted freely about their political aims, they made it quite obvious that they were in deadly earnest and produced explosives, threatening to blow up the plane if there were any hint of disobedience on anyone's part.

Captain Ishida brought the Boeing down at Fukuoka where the hijackers allowed twenty-three of the passengers to get off. The remainder were forced to remain in their seats while the plane refuelled. Police who had been summoned to meet the plane were ordered to keep their distance. None of them dared approach nearer than twenty yards and they were powerless to act. A genuine technical fault kept the plane grounded until two o'clock in the afternoon. Then Ishida took off for North Korea, shadowed at a safe distance by Japanese and American military aircraft.

By this time the Japanese and Korean authorities had been thoroughly alerted. No time had been lost in raiding the headquarters of the Red Army organization in Tokyo, Osaka, and other cities. Some arrests were made and sheafs of documents confiscated. Meanwhile, Captain Ishida was heading north towards the 38th Parallel – the frontier between South Korea and Communist North Korea. But unknown to the hijackers, Ishida, instead of crossing the Parallel, veered off in the direction of Seoul, capital of South Korea. There the authorities had concocted an elaborate hoax. From the top of the Kimpo terminal building they had hung North Korean flags and Communist streamers. The

name of the airport had been obliterated. The ground crew
had been dressed in nondescript overalls and a contingent of
soldiers was ready on parade, specially fitted out with North
Korean Army uniforms. In this way the South Korean
authorities hoped to fool the hijackers into believing that
they had in fact touched down at Pyongyang. Once they
stepped off the plane they would all be arrested.

When the Boeing landed at Seoul, it seemed for a while
that the students had been taken in by the ruse. But the
passengers were still refused permission to leave while the
hijackers spoke to the Korean officials. As the minutes
ticked away it was obvious that they were becoming sus-
picious. Finally they turned the tables on their would-be
captors. They fired off some obscure questions on points of
Communist doctrine, which left the officials stammering and
utterly confused. The students then realized they had been
tricked and headed back for the plane, demanding to be
flown on to Pyongyang and again threatening to blow up the
plane if there were any further delaying tactics.

Captain Ishida, however, had allowed for the possible
failure of the ruse. On landing, he had deliberately overshot
the tarmac and buried the nose wheel of the Boeing in the
soft grass alongside the runway. It would need a ground
crew to pry the wheel loose and prepare the plane for take-
off. This gave the authorities time to begin negotiations.
They had already telephoned Tokyo to send out a relief
crew, arguing that it would be unsafe for Captain Ishida to
continue at the controls after his long ordeal. They also
offered to hand over hostages, including a Japanese Government minister and the ambassador to South Korea in exchange for the passengers and crew. The students refused.
The unfortunate passengers were kept prisoners, by now
desperate for fresh air, food, and drink, some of them near to
fainting, all through that Tuesday night and for two more
days and nights. Although there was still no violence shown
to any of them, many were in full agreement with one of
their number who, when interviewed later, described it 'like
in hell'.

All through the Wednesday and Thursday the negotiations went on, by this time in the full glare of Press and television coverage. The Japanese were encouraged by the news that the North Korean Government had officially refused their cooperation to the hijackers. They promised that once the plane arrived in Pyongyang it would be guarded and then returned to its rightful owners. The safety of the crew and passengers would also be guaranteed.

By now the endurance of the nine students was beginning to wear thin. When the Japanese Deputy Minister of Transport boarded the plane and offered to remain as hostage, together with three crew members, the hijackers finally agreed to release the weary passengers. On Friday morning they were allowed off the plane, in two batches, after spending seventy-nine hours in captivity. Later they were flown back home unharmed to rejoin anxious relatives and friends. The Boeing then took off for Pyongyang, where the North Koreans gave it a frosty reception, complaining that it had not received permission to land. It was duly returned to Tokyo as promised, but the nine Red Army students were allowed to stay in North Korea.

So ended one of the most astonishing hijacking attempts of modern times. Only exemplary patience and courage on the part of captain, crew, and passengers prevented it from ending in tragedy.

24

The Arab Guerrillas

Ordeal in the Desert

'Free the prisoners you are holding or we blow up the planes, their crews, and all the passengers on board!' This was the grim message flashed through to the Governments of five nations on a September day in 1970. It was a threat which posed a cruel decision for the Governments concerned and which shocked civilized people all over the world.

The message came from the leaders of a fanatical Arab guerrilla organization. The three airliners involved were a Swissair DC-8, a Boeing 707, and a BOAC VC-10. On board were a total of 439 passengers, most of them American, British, German, or Swiss. It was the lives of these passengers that were at stake.

This bold skyjacking operation was the work of a group of Palestinians who made it clear that they regarded it as part of the continuing war between the Arab states and Israel. But, unlike other commando groups, they made it equally clear that they were prepared to hold as hostages and even kill innocent men, women, and children who were in no way involved in this conflict.

It was a cleverly executed plan and the timing was perfect. Yet things did not go as smoothly as the hijackers had hoped. The first plane on their list was the American TWA Boeing, with 149 passengers and ten crew members on board. It had just taken off from Frankfurt and was crossing the West German–Belgian border when two men held up the crew at gun point and ordered the captain to change course across the Mediterranean to Jordan. Since the country was on the verge of civil war, the plane could not land at the main airport of Amman and was diverted to a secluded airstrip in the desert known as Dawson's Field. The guerrillas called it Revolution Airfield.

Barely two hours later, a Swissair DC-7 bound from Zurich to New York was similarly hijacked over France and flown to Jordan, touching down safely alongside the American airliner. On board were 155 people, including the crew.

The exultant guerrillas proudly announced their double achievement to the world and threatened to hold crews and passengers hostage until certain demands were met. Meanwhile, however, the third stage of the operation had badly misfired. This called for the hijacking of an Israeli El Al Boeing 707, bound from Israel to New York. The plane had made a transit stop in Amsterdam and was over the North Sea, approaching the English coast, when a man and a girl leapt from their seats, brandishing pistols. The man rushed towards the cockpit but was intercepted by a steward. A shot was fired and the steward collapsed, wounded in the stomach. The captain, who had been warned immediately of trouble, sent the plane into a sudden dive in order to lose height and reduce the pressure level. It threw the hijacker off balance and he was shot dead by an armed security officer. A grenade which he dropped on the floor fortunately proved to be a dud.

Meanwhile, the girl produced two grenades from beneath her clothes; but before she could draw out the pins she was overpowered and trussed up by a passenger and the stewards. Shortly afterwards the plane landed safely at London airport. The girl, identified as Leila Khaled, already wanted for another hijacking episode, was taken into custody.

By a stroke of irony, the unsuccessful attempt on the El Al plane led to a fourth hijacking. Although officials at Amsterdam failed to recognize Leila and her companion, they did stop two other suspicious-looking men boarding the same plane. The men, who carried Senegalese passports,

were allowed to take an alternative flight on a Pan Am
Boeing 747, the new Jumbo Jet. Three-quarters of an hour
after the giant airliner took off for New York, a stewardess
found a pistol levelled at her head and the captain was
ordered to alter course for the south. He was given permission to land at Beirut airport in the Lebanon, where
another group of armed guerrillas, one carrying a suitcase
full of dynamite, swarmed aboard. Now the captain was
commanded to take the plane on to Cairo, where the crew
and passengers were hastily disembarked through emergency exists. Within minutes the huge aeroplane was blown
into fragments. It was a warning of what might happen to
the other planes if the guerrillas did not get their way.

The hijackers had not yet completed their plans. Several
days later the fifth plane, a BOAC VC-10, bound from Bah-
rein to London, with 114 passengers and crew, was hijacked
over the Persian Gulf. It refuelled at Beirut, in full view of
newspapermen and television cameramen. Then it went on
to join the other two airliners on the lonely desert airstrip in
Jordan.

Now the guerrillas outlined their terms. All the hostages
would be held captive inside the planes until a number of
their arrested or imprisoned comrades were set free. They
included Leila Khaled, six guerrillas in West Germany and
Switzerland serving sentences for terrorist crimes, and an
unspecified number of guerrillas captured and held in
Israel.

The five Governments concerned knew that they were
being blackmailed but could afford to take no chances. The
Cairo episode had proved that the guerrillas would not hesitate to blow up the planes, but this time the passengers' lives
were also at risk. They acted cautiously, using the International Red Cross to negotiate on their behalf, making it
clear that they were acting together and would only do a
deal provided all the hostages were released.

While the negotiations went on, under increasingly
dangerous and confusing conditions, the unfortunate passengers waited in their planes, surrounded by a ring of armed

guerrillas. They knew from what their captors told them and from the news on their transistor radios that their lives were in terrible danger. But all of them, men, women, and children, remained calm. They were not ill-treated, but conditions grew steadily worse. It was stiflingly hot by day and cruelly cold at night. Food and water were in short supply and the air-conditioning systems were not functioning. Time passed, and they were given additional food and drinks by the guerrillas. Emergency air-conditioning plants were installed and sanitary conditions improved. But as each new ultimatum deadline grew near, their fears increased. The worst moment came as they watched the guerrillas placing dynamite charges below their planes. Although they were allowed out of the planes briefly for exercise, the guerrillas stuck to their threat. No further delays would be tolerated. Unless their Arab comrades were immediately freed, the planes and their occupants would be blown to smithereens.

But the firm front presented by the Governments and the pressure of public opinion throughout the world eventually forced the guerrillas to reconsider. Just before the last deadline expired they announced that they would free all the women and children on board. Almost a hundred people were taken to a hotel in Amman and later released. Shortly afterwards, the remaining passengers and crew members were herded off the planes. Then, as they watched from a safe distance, the three airliners were blown up one by one, the swirling columns of black smoke being clearly visible twenty miles away.

The world breathed a sigh of relief. Although three planes worth ten million pounds had been blown up, the passengers were safe. But were they? The story was not yet over. For although the guerrillas had now released almost 400 of the hostages, they had kept back another fifty-four and whisked them away to a secret hideout. As the Governments continued their feverish negotiations, threats to the missing hostages' lives increased daily as full-scale civil war erupted in Jordan.

For more than a week there was no further news of them. Then, as the guerrillas abandoned their strongholds to Government troops after fierce fighting, the first batch of hostages – British, Swiss, and West German – were rescued from a building in which they had been held captive. The following day the remaining American hostages were also handed over by the guerrillas. Once again, by a combination of good sense and good luck, a hijacking tragedy had narrowly been averted.

Yet the uncomfortable fact remained that nothing had been solved. The air pirates were still at large. Sooner or later they would strike again.